Electric Money:
Evolution of
an Electronic
Funds-Transfer
System

The MIT Press
Cambridge, Massachusetts
and London, England

Electric Money:
Evolution of
an Electronic
Funds-Transfer
System

Dennis W.
Richardson

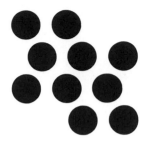

Set in
Linotype Baskerville
Printed and bound
in the United States of
America by
The Colonial Press Inc.

ISBN 0 262 18045 6
(hardcover)

Library of Congress
catalog card number:
74-110233

Foreword

Prominent in the economic literature of the 1960s was the controversy concerning the importance, linkage, and ultimate impact of changes in the money supply on economic activity. That money does indeed matter is no longer a question in the arena of economic discussion: the monetarists have won their point. However, the pace of innovation in the American economy is such that one of the important monetary issues of the 1970s will be the impact upon the money supply and the economy of the complete automation of the payments mechanism. It is ironic that a move to an electronic funds-transfer system may destroy much of the framework erected by the monetarists by changing the structure of our money system and even the definition of money.

The publication of *Electric Money: Evolution of an Electronic Funds-Transfer System* by Dennis W. Richardson helps fill a substantial void in the literature on monetary structure and banking practice. Much of the published material on the payments system so far has been couched in a "checkless society" framework. The best — but not all — of it avoided the science fiction approach that describes in infinite detail the wonders of the new system and how wondrous it will be when completely operational.

Unfortunately, not as much effort has been devoted to an analysis of why and how such a new system might develop and to an evaluation of the dramatic change in institutional characteristics of the money system that would follow such an innovation. Even less thought has been given to the dramatic changes in monetary policy that must accompany a change to an automated payments system. Dr. Richardson not only provides much of the institutional knowledge needed by those who would seek to understand the revolution in our money system, but also offers reasons why and how it will occur.

Dr. Richardson is particularly qualified to write on the coming innovations in the payments mechanism. He has written a number of articles and monographs on the phenomenal growth of the bank credit card and on technological changes in banking and their impact on the banking system. For some time he has been a consultant to the Economics Task Force of the Monetary and Payments System Planning

Committee of The American Bankers Association, which has mounted an intensive investigation into the meaning to the commercial banking system of the prospective change to an electronic funds-transfer system.

Commercial bankers who have been searching for a concise text on the evolution of the payments system toward complete automation should find this book both an excellent reference and a path to the knowledge they need. Those who have a particular interest in financial institutions that compete with commercial banks in the various financial markets will discover many new thoughts relevant to their position vis-à-vis banks. But the book will be most useful to the student of the money and banking system. The early chapters on the evolution of the money system bring together many scattered references that describe how and why the money system functions. The chapters on the present system of payment media, the nonbank credit card, the bank credit card, and the preauthorized payment system present material that will be new and useful to the most advanced money student.

Despite the interest in the early chapters that develop the characteristics of the present payments system, the basic message of the book begins with the introduction and description of a possible electronic funds-transfer system. The contribution that is unique to the book includes Chapters Eight and Nine, which contain the author's conclusions as to the implications for the commercial banking industry, other industries, and monetary policy itself of the development of a system for the electronic transfer of funds. Here, in a few pages, the advantages and disadvantages of such a system for the commercial banking system are examined. The position of the principal competitors, such as savings and loan associations, insurance companies, and savings banks, to commercial banks is compared. Finally, the role of monetary policy is examined in an attempt to determine how the Federal Reserve System might respond to the gradual introduction of the electronic funds-transfer system.

If one is interested in the character and function of a radically different monetary system that is likely to confront not only students of money and banking but also — a sobering thought — a mass of untrained or ill-trained people in their role as "personal money managers," one should read this book.

Herbert E. Johnson
Vice President, Planning and Development
Continental Bank
Chicago, Illinois

Preface

There was much talk during the latter half of the decade of the sixties concerning the prospects of a "checkless" or even "cashless-checkless" society. After some of the initial exuberance subsided, the more popular phrase became "less-cash, less-checks" society. By all indications this later terminology should be considered more accurate, since even today barter has not been eliminated completely.

In this book I have chosen to use the phrase "electronic funds-transfer system" to mean a future state of society wherein a majority of the payments transfers is made via electronic (or automated) transfer systems. The approach taken is to view "electronic money" as the next logical step in a rather long, evolutionary development of payment media in general.

Most of the basic research for this book was completed by the early part of 1968. But since the approach is generic, I believe that the basic trends, institutional arrangements, and time projections stated in it have been supported by developments during the last two years.

The most meaningful developments recently have been the specific planning for, and the actual emergence of, regional computer centers. For example, the Omniswitch Corporation began operations in New York in November, 1969. The Omniswitch is a bank-owned credit verification system which was organized originally to contend with credit verification problems of the two large credit-card systems in New York: the First National City Bank and the Eastern States Bankcard Association (ESBA). Membership in the Omniswitch is open to any firm engaged in a charge-card or credit-card operation which has switch authorization centers capable of receiving incoming Omniswitch authorization inquiries and generating automated authorization responses. Plans are for the Omniswitch to provide automated sales authorization services on a national scale. At the time of this writing serious discussions are underway for the formation of a national charge-card fraud-control communications network by officials of American Express and Bank-Americard. The proposed venture would result in two corporations owned jointly by American Express and BankAmericard: the National Authorization Services Corporation would be a nonprofit membership group, and the National Authorization Systems Corporation would operate the network.

Perhaps the most significant step toward electronic funds transference occurred in California in April, 1968. During this month the San Francisco and Los Angeles Clearing House Associations authorized the creation of a special joint committee to study and recommend arrangements for exchanging "paperless" credits and debits between banks. The Special Committee on "Paperless" Entries (SCOPE) has been making specific recommendations for exchanging (1) automatic credits via magnetic tape, punch cards, or deposit tickets; (2) automatic debits via magnetic tape or punch cards; and (3) magnetic tape accompanying normal clearing checks. With the cooperation of the leading California banks and the San Francisco Federal Reserve Bank, automated clearing facilities will soon be in operation. Very recently six commercial banks in Seattle have begun investigating a SCOPE system, and other groups of banks around the country are expected to initiate SCOPE projects of their own.

The completion of this study would have been impossible without the exchange of ideas which occurred during interviews and attendance at many meetings, workshops, and conferences related to recent innovations in the payments and credit system. I owe a debt of gratitude to the American Bankers Association, which sponsored my attendance to its National Credit-Card Conference in Chicago, November, 1967; Preauthorized Payments Workshop in New Orleans, January, 1968; and National Automation Conference in Bal Harbour, Florida, May, 1968.

In particular, acknowledgment is due the following individuals who from presentations or informal discussion provided many insights into the course of development and possible implications of an evolving electronic monetary system: Dr. Thomas R. Atkinson, Director, Department of Economics and Research, The American Bankers Association; Mr. Charles Block, Vice President, The Chase Manhattan Bank, N.A.; Mr. John J. Clarke, Vice President and Special Legal Adviser, Federal Reserve Bank of New York; Mr. James K. Dobey, Executive Vice President, Wells Fargo Bank; Mr. H. B. Hassinger, Executive Vice President, The First National Bank of Boston; Dr. Herbert E. Johnson, Vice President, Continental Illinois National Bank; Dr. Eugene Lerner, Professor of Finance, Northwestern University; Mr. Putnam Livingston, Vice President, Bankers Trust Company; and Mr. Dale L. Reistad, President, Payment Systems Inc.

I am indebted especially to Mr. Ed R. L. Wroe, Jr., President, American National Bank, Austin, Texas, who lent his support to this project when it was in its earliest stage of development. Invaluable support and assistance were provided by my good friend, Dr. Lawrence L. Crum, Professor and Chairman, Department of Finance; and Director, Research Program in Banking Innovations, The University of Texas at Austin. I relied heavily on Dr. Crum's knowledge of the banking industry, and he made many valuable suggestions and criticisms when reading earlier drafts of the entire manuscript. Since I exercised free choice in accepting or not accepting any suggestions made, of course, the responsibility for what the book lacks is mine.

D. W. R.
Austin, Texas
May, 1970

Tables

Table

Illustrations

Figure

Electric Money:
Evolution of
an Electronic
Funds-Transfer
System

Recent technological developments in the areas of microelectronics, electronic data processing, and information retrieval and communications systems will revolutionize the American monetary system. The technical advancements that currently are being implemented by progressive bankers are on the verge of completely changing the traditional concepts of payment media and commercial banking. The officers of many large banks and some officials of the Federal Reserve System and the American Bankers Association already envision the elimination of what we now use for money, long-distance banking by remote tellers, banks' automatic payment of customers' reoccurring bills, automatic deposit and loan services, and preauthorized, computer-programed investment portfolios as part of the everyday services offered by the commercial bank of tomorrow.

In the not-too-distant future, money usage as it is known today largely will have disappeared, and the intricate process of settlement and deposit accounting will be conducted concurrently at and between two hundred to three hundred regional computer centers located throughout the country. The process will operate like a modified giro system, where the payor initiates the settlement process, but does so by communicating with his bank, not the payee. Under a fully implemented electronic funds-transfer system, deposit balances will be transferred instantaneously to any area of the country by means of electronic impulses.

If the prognostications advanced here appear unrealistic, let the reply to any skepticism be that nearly all of the innovations alluded to in the previous paragraphs are already in existence and in limited operation. Of course, the transition from present payment media to a future electronic funds-transfer system will not occur overnight. In the United States there are close to fourteen thousand commercial banks, nearly two million retail establishments, and over sixty million household units which eventually must become committed to the concept of a "cashless-checkless" society. The period of transition will be measured in years; however, citizens, bankers, businessmen, government officials, and monetary authorities' decisions in the very near future will need to reflect the many changes during the period of development of a "computerized" monetary system. It is the evolution toward a future electronic funds-transfer system and the implications of such a system that form the central hypothesis and subject of the present study.

1.1. The Nature of Innovation in Payment Media Systems

Innovation is more than the development of new ideas and their implementation; it also involves new attitudes toward change. While the old stereotype of the banker reluctant to entertain new ideas was never entirely justified, many commercial bankers in recent years have developed a much more aggressive spirit of management. These same bankers are implementing the latest technological innovations and actively marketing new bank services. By virtue of the commercial banking system's central position in the payments mechanism, these developments will affect almost all financial transactions.

At the present time approximately 90 percent of the dollar volume of transactions in the United States are consummated with the use of the check. Last year over eighteen billion checks were written by Americans; the value of these transactions was close to four trillion dollars. And these figures are increasing at a rate between 6 and 7 percent annually. A good portion of the work in a modern commercial bank is that entailed in handling checks. It is estimated that each check on the average is transferred ten times. The elaborate organization for controlling the flow of checks not only consists of individual banks' bookkeeping departments but it also consists of the facilities of local clearinghouses, correspondent banks, and the Federal Reserve System. For the banking system, the annual cost of handling checks is estimated to be nearly three and one-half billion dollars. It would appear that the check as the major means of debt settlement has created a situation ready made for the application of electronic data-processing technology. There is an impressive need to innovate a new medium of payment.

There have been only four major innovations in payment media systems in history: (1) the barter system, the origin of which is buried in antiquity; (2) the use of full-bodied money and eventually metal coinage, which developed around the seventh century B.C.; (3) the use as a medium of ownership of written receipts, the forerunners of paper money, introduced by the goldsmiths and earliest banks in the Middle Ages; and finally (4) the use of checks, which were first used in the United States in 1681.

At the present time "money" is used ultimately for the settlement of nearly all debts. Money is part of the framework of the economy, and many aspects of human behavior are built around this framework. If the monetary system changes, other things are affected, even if the connections among them are not readily seen. Because of the important functions money performs, it affects economic activity in a variety of ways that are related yet distinct. Money not only touches all aspects of the functioning economy, it is the intermediary through which Americans transmit most decisions about production, consumption, and the vast majority of economic matters.

To the modern economist, money is a social device that serves in many ways to increase economic productivity. At one time, money was thought of as little more than a passive medium used to achieve economic ends. Today, however, most economists agree that money itself can influence the real aspects of the economy. Through payments of money, the products and services that are the real end result of the economic process move from producers to ultimate consumers. Production, income, and welfare are influenced by changes in the stock of money and changes in the rate of speed with which money moves from one person or institution to another.

In addition to the economic aspects of human behavior that money influences, there are also social and psychological aspects. Today, there are many emotional attitudes that arise due to the social character of money. Not only are people concerned with what money will buy. They are concerned with money as an index of prestige, social status, security, and achievement. For many years Americans have associated money with a physical object either in coin, currency, or checkbook form. Psychologically, people have developed certain attitudes and patterns of behavior associated with specific forms of money with which they are familiar. Psychologists have found that individuals from middle-class families, more than individuals from other social classes, exhibit frustration manifested by dreams of finding money. Experiments have shown that coins appear larger in size to children from poor families than they do to children from more prosperous backgrounds.

Psychological and social attitudes cannot be ignored since the ways that people feel about money have important implications for the way they permit it to perform its utilitarian functions. Between the sixteenth and nineteenth centuries, for example, monetary policies were greatly influenced by semimystical attitudes toward money. Bullionism led entire nations to subordinate their national economic goals to the accumulation of precious metals. In recent years, however, we have progressed further and further away from the notion that money must have some sort of "intrinsic worth."

The legal environment in which the banking and monetary systems operate exerts a powerful influence on the structure of institutions and the implementation of new developments. Two years after the National Currency Act was passed in 1863, it was thought that this act had taxed the state banks out of existence by a punitive 10 percent levy on state bank notes. But the state banks survived by aggressively implementing the innovation previously referred to as checking accounts and demand deposits. Even though checks were introduced almost two centuries earlier, it was the passage of legislation that motivated the state banking system to promote the acceptance of the check as a major medium of exchange.

The nature of innovation in payment media systems is an extremely complex phenomenon having implications for nearly all sectors of the economy. Major innovations often are precipitated by a series of smaller developments. In recent years the stock of money has not been increasing as rapidly as the volume of transactions. This is partly because charge accounts, credit cards, bank credit cards, preauthorized payments, and other media have facilitated the use of short-term credit and greater monetary velocity. These developments represent key factors to be considered in a study of the next major innovation in payment media systems, an electronic funds-transfer system.

1.2. Statement of Need and Purpose

Computer and electronics technology is on the verge of completely changing the nature of many existing economic concepts and financial institutions. Innovations in technology are not only impressive from a technical point of view, but their major impact arises from the "chain reaction" of effects on industry, education, and society. It has been said that technological change is the most powerful factor in the American business environment today. In such a mercurial atmosphere, traditional business methodology, pedagogical techniques, and social institutions are made obsolete in a matter of a few years. There is no certain way of facing the problems introduced by large-scale innovations, but businessmen and educators must become more skillful in dealing with environmental changes by anticipating their effects, planning, training, and adapting successfully.

The need of business and industrial leaders for advanced information on future technical developments and innovations cannot be overstated. In recent years the degree of success of a business enterprise has been determined to a large extent by the ability of its managers to respond effectively to these changes. Insights into the impact of electronic money transference must be provided to business managers today in order for them to meet successfully the problems of tomorrow.

What is needed now is an exploratory research study designed to identify and evaluate the current and potential influences which will effect the development and implementation of an electronic funds-transfer system. This study will apply the lessons of history and contemporary knowledge of money, credit, and financial institutions within a framework of socioeconomic theory to analyze recent developments leading toward a future "cashless-checkless" society. It will be important for this project to specify the significant and far-reaching effects of electronic funds transference on commercial banking and other industries which are heavily committed to various forms of credit transactions and operations in financial markets. This study will reveal some of the potential implications of a "computerized" monetary system for the current concept of "money," monetary velocity, the demand for money, and monetary policies aimed toward economic stabilization. It is also the purpose of this study to generate hypotheses, identify potential problems, and indicate areas for additional research.

1.3. Organization of the Study

While it is true that the American monetary and banking systems are experiencing a considerable amount of innovation at the present time, current innovation is only one more step in the long history of change in financial institutions and financial structure. A look at the past should provide many insights into the future. Accordingly, Chapter 2 begins with an examination of the evolution of innovation in payment media systems. Because every society will have developed during the course of evolution a unique set of institutions, laws, and customs that distinguishes its financial system from all others, it is important to present in Chapter 3 a more detailed description of the development of the monetary and banking systems of the United States. This record provides the foundation for an analysis of the current system of payment media in the United States, which is presented in Chapter 4. In this chapter the concept of payment media is broadened to include the recent and extensive use of credit to facilitate economic activity. Many of the latest financial developments have been directed toward the promotion of a greater utilization of credit in consummating transactions. One of these new devices is the credit card. The credit card represents a significant development by itself as a means of facilitating the payments mechanism. But it is of even greater importance to this study because electronic funds transference in all probability will be activated by a card similar to but more advanced than the bank credit cards now being issued in large numbers.

Chapter 5 is an analysis of the evolution and current status of the nonbank credit card. Besides indicating the major reasons for development and present volume and degree of utilization of nonbank credit cards, this chapter considers in some detail the costs and problems experienced by credit-card issuers. The two major developments that have motivated recent speculations of a future "cashless-checkless" society are analyzed in Chapter 6; these are bank credit cards and pre-authorized payment systems. These two developments in a more advanced state of implementation will lead the progression toward a future electronic funds-transfer system.

The first section of Chapter 7 is devoted to the construction of a theoretical model of a society without the benefits of a medium of exchange; its purpose is to establish the logical feasibility for the elimination of what we now use for money.

The second section of this volume presents a description of a hypothetical electronic funds-transfer system as it might evolve within the real-world constraints of financial, social, and economic variables. Chapters 8 and 9 are predicated on the assumption of a commercial bank-centered electronic funds-transfer system. Within this conceptual framework the former chapter presents an analysis of implications for commercial banking and other industries. The latter chapter presents the implications of electronic funds transference for monetary theory as they may affect economic stabilization policies. Chapter 10 contains the summary and conclusions of the study.

Innovation means renewal — improving old capabilities as new methods
and ideas are accepted and eventually replace old ones. Innovation is
not a simple action; it is a total evolutionary process with many inter-
related parts. It is not just the discovery or development of a new
phenomenon; it is also, and perhaps more importantly, the implementation of a new phenomenon. Meaningful innovation is the utilization of
new concepts and methods in such a way as to achieve the goals of
society. Depending upon the value system of a particular group or
society a new development may be accepted and readily implemented
or rejected and quickly forgotten.

This chapter will be concerned with the evolution of innovation in
payment media systems and will attempt to establish three logically
distinct stages in the development of exchange media. It will not be
suggested that these stages can be precisely divided chronologically,
because there are societies in the world in which each of these stages of
exchange can be found today. In even the most sophisticated and advanced economies a prior stage does not pass entirely out of existence
when a succeeding one becomes predominant.

The three stages of development with which this chapter will be
concerned are (1) barter, (2) full-bodied money, and (3) representative
and credit money. Because the major focus of this study is on future
developments in payment media systems, it will be helpful to divide the
last stage into two subsystems in the innovative process: (a) state-issued
representative and credit money, and (b) bank-issued representative and
credit money.

2.1. The Concept of "Money"

Prior to a discussion of the evolution of payment media systems, it
should be helpful to investigate the concept of "money."

Aristotle in the *Ethics* speaks of the functions of money: "It is therefore indispensable that all things which can be exchanged should be
capable of comparison, and for this purpose money has come in, and
comes to be a kind of medium, for it measures all things and so likewise the excess and defect . . . ; the need as was stated above of some

one measure of all things." [1] It appears quite clear that Aristotle considers it essential that money possesses what has more recently been referred to as the primary functions of money — the medium-of-exchange function and the standard-of-value function. He was the first to call money a "medium of exchange" and to describe its function as a standard of value.[2]

The study of money as a distinct area of economics probably had its foundation in the writings of scholars in the latter eighteenth and early nineteenth centuries. In his *Inquiry into the Nature and Causes of the Wealth of Nations,* Adam Smith spoke of money in his discussion of division of labor, saying:

But when the division of labour first began to take place, this power of exchanging must frequently have been very much clogged and embarrassed in its operations. One man, we shall suppose has more of a certain commodity than he himself has occasion for, while another has less. The former consequently would be glad to dispose of, and the latter to purchase, a part of this superfluity. But if this latter should chance to have nothing that the former stands in need of, no exchange can be made between them . . . In order to avoid the inconveniency of such situations, every prudent man in every period of society, after the first establishment of the division of labour, must naturally have endeavored to manage his affairs in such a manner, as to have at all times by him, besides the peculiar produce of his own industry, a certain quantity of some one commodity or other such as he imagined few people would be likely to refuse in exchange for the produce of their industry.[3]

Apparently in Smith's mind the medial nature of money was foremost. His treatment on the nature and functions of money, however, is anything but extensive. Later noted economists added refinements and elaborated on other functions which money performs. These economists established the foundation upon which contemporary writers have built their definitions of money. Textbook writers for the most part have taken an eclectic approach in formulating concise definitions of money and enumerating its functions. They have relied on the writings of monetary economists before them and have attempted to integrate the best aspects of each. Several of the definitions in contemporary textbooks on money and banking will be considered here.

Without giving a precise definition of money, Lester V. Chandler writes, "We may say, then, that the sole purpose of money in the economic system is to enable trade to be carried on as cheaply as

[1] Richard McKeon (ed.), *The Basic Works of Aristotle* (New York: Random House, 1941), Book 5, Chapter 8.
[2] Rupert J. Ederer, *The Evolution of Money* (Washington, D.C.: Public Affairs Press, 1964), p. 7.
[3] Adam Smith, *The Wealth of Nations* (New York: Modern Library Edition), p. 22.

possible in order to make feasible the optimum degree of specialization, with its attendant increase of productivity." Even though Chandler does not actually define money, he is very emphatic about its primary function. He stresses that "Money has but one fundamental purpose in an economic system: to facilitate the exchange of goods and services — to lessen the time and effort required to carry on trade." [4]

It is interesting to note that Charles L. Prather in his sixth edition of *Money and Banking* presents the following definition of money: "In modern economics, money is anything which is customarily used as a medium of exchange or means of payment and as a standard of value." However, in his eighth, and latest edition that definition is no longer presented. Instead he appears to let the reader form his own definition after a discussion of the role of money in a capitalistic society. He writes:

Money is a social tool whose origin is buried in antiquity. How it is used reflects the type of society in which one lives, being most important in a free enterprise society wherein production for the market-place dominates. For such an economy, it is imperative to have a medium of exchange, a store of value, and a standard of deferred payments; because sooner or later, money is spent for goods and services including the settlement of debts and taxes. [5]

In his later edition Prather tends to emphasize the social value of money and discusses its functions in a broader context than in the earlier edition.

Raymond P. Kent defines money "as anything that is commonly used and generally accepted as a medium of exchange or as a standard of value." He qualifies this definition by reminding the reader of the difficulty of ascribing a precise definition to a complex concept such as money, and continues for several paragraphs to refine and explain it. One important difference stands out in his definition, however, when compared with many others. He emphasizes:

. . . money is used as a medium of exchange *or* as a standard of value. Thus we classify as money anything that is commonly used and generally accepted as a medium of exchange even though it does not serve as a standard of value, and we also recognize as money anything that is commonly used and generally accepted as a standard of value even though it is not employed as a medium of exchange. [6]

In the early nineteenth century it was customary among economists to produce extensive lists of the many functions of money. Today,

[4] Lester V. Chandler, *The Economics of Money and Banking* (New York: Harper, 1959), p. 2.

[5] Charles L. Prather, *Money and Banking* (Homewood. Ill.: Richard D. Irwin, 1965), 6th ed., p. 1; 8th ed, p. 6.

[6] Raymond P. Kent, *Money and Banking* (New York: Holt, Rinehart and Winston, 1966), 5th ed., p. 4.

perhaps due to the writings of Wicksell, monetary theorists tend to reduce these functions into two primary ones. Included as the primary functions are a medium of exchange and a standard of value. Among the secondary functions are included a means of deferred payment and a store of value.

So far, the discussion on the concept of money has centered mostly around *the functions of money* rather than *what is money*, and it appears that recent writers in the field of money and banking also have ignored this latter point. Perhaps as money has evolved over time it becomes increasingly futile to attempt to define money by its material substance. This emphasis on the primary functions of money was stated adroitly by R. G. Hawtrey when he said:

Money is one of those concepts which, like a teaspoon or an umbrella, but unlike an earth quake or a buttercup, are definable primarily by the use or purpose which they serve. The use or purpose of money is twofold: it provides a medium of exchange and a measure of value.[7]

Today, the bulk of what we use as money does not exist in form but in concept. In 1950, A. C. Pigou made the following observation:

A pound sterling is not a thing at all. It is a name handed down in history. It is open to the government to proclaim at any time that a coin constituted in such-and-such a way, or a paper note on which such-and-such a device is printed or, if it should so choose, a peach or a strawberry — is equivalent to a pound sterling; so that debts falling due, that were contracted in terms of sterling are legally acquitted by a transfer from debtor to creditor of the appropriate number of these things.[8]

We may conclude from the foregoing discussion that "money is what money does." It will be of only historical interest to specify the physical form which money has taken, and as was pointed out earlier, through the evolution of payment media money has come to be for the most part a *concept* and to an increasingly lesser extent a *thing*. Consequently, we can rely heavily on money's fundamental purpose as described by Chandler, "to facilitate the exchange of goods and services — to lessen the time and effort required to carry on trade."

2.2. Barter Systems

To barter means to trade, to exchange goods or services for other goods or services. A barter transaction is different from a money transaction in that when the former is made, the exchange of goods or services is made with the purpose of obtaining simultaneously the respective "use value" of the goods or services exchanged. Thus, under a barter system a seller of a commodity must not only find someone

[7] R. G. Hawtrey, *Currency and Credit* (London: Longmans, Green, 1950), 4th ed., p. 1.
[8] A. C. Pigou, *The Veil of Money* (London: Macmillan, 1950), pp. 4–5.

who is willing to give value for his commodity, but someone who is also willing to give in exchange some article that the seller wishes to acquire.[9] When a monetary unit is introduced, however, the dual coincidence of wants is not necessary, and the exchange may be separated into two transactions in time.

Barter as a commonly used system of exchange existed in prehistoric time; we can, however, make some generalizations about these systems from historians' descriptions of partial barter after the fall of the Roman Empire and from anthropologists' studies of primitive cultures in existence in present times.

Many monetary historians have contended that there are two prerequisites for any kind of exchange system, including barter: (1) private property and (2) division of labor. Since it is not possible to verify empirically whether or not private property and division of labor are necessary for exchange, we can only speculate about the origin of barter. Paul Einzig states that,

Primitive religion provides a strong motive for barter before the development of either private property or division of labour. The innumerable variety of temporary or permanent taboos imposed on the groups is apt to lead to the exchange of the products affected against products which the tribesmen are entitled to consume. Totemism leads to exchanges between the various totemic groups.[10]

There appears to be little doubt, however, that barter was the earliest form of exchange; barter formed the foundation for the development of markets where the concepts of *value* and *price* emerged. At one time it was thought that various forms of barter evolved into money systems, where a particular type of commodity most generally bartered came to serve as a common medium of exchange. However, it is difficult to reconcile such an explanation with the known adoption of many monetary units. The ox of Homeric Greece or the elephant of Ceylon could hardly have become a commonly accepted medium of exchange. Rather it is believed that money originated out of certain social customs, in particular religious ritual.

Barter, according to anthropologists, was not as prevalent within social groups as it was among such groups. Internal group exchanges were most often social and ceremonial gift-giving, whereas intergroup barter served as a means of meeting economic wants. An interesting example of intergroup exchange is so-called "silent trade." Silent trade refers to a process of exchange where no direct contact occurs between the parties to the transaction. Members of a particular group would leave items at a designated place, and individuals of a second

[9] W. T. Newlyn, *Theory of Money* (Oxford: Clarendon Press, 1962), p. 1.
[10] Paul Einzig, *Primitive Money* (London: Eyre-Spottiswoode, 1949), p. 348.

group would come and if they desired the items they would leave different goods in their stead. Examples of silent trade have been reported by Herodotus and Ibn Battuta in medieval times. Silent trade has also been found by modern anthropologists to exist among certain Indian tribes in California, Pygmies and Bantus in the Congo, and natives in New Guinea.

As man's curiosity grew and as relations with neighboring tribes permitted friendly intercourse with one another, open barter replaced silent trade. It would seem logical that bargaining accompanying a barter exchange would eventually lead to more or less fixed exchange ratios among tribes which customarily traded. There are many examples of rigidly established exchange ratios. As late as 2 A.D. the ancient Irish employed this table:

8 wheat grains equal 1 pin ginn of silver
3 pin ginns equal 1 screpall
3 screpalls equal 1 sheep
4 sheep equal 1 heifer
6 heifers equal 1 cow
3 cows equal 1 kumal (slave girl)[11]

Throughout history barter has appeared frequently as a retrogression. When such a phenomenon occurred, in most cases the last known monetary unit was used as a standard of value. Under a barter system, one of the greatest impediments to trade is the lack of a common denominator to which the value of a variety of goods and services can be compared. A brief discussion of the major disadvantages of barter may be helpful for purposes of reference later on.

According to Lester V. Chandler the shortcomings of barter constitute the only reason for the invention and use of money. In his treatise on money, he describes at some length the disadvantages of barter. He states, "The first serious shortcoming of pure barter . . . is the lack of any common unit in terms of which to measure and state the values of goods and services." [12] Under barter the value of each good and service cannot be stated simply in terms of one quantity. Every article would have to be stated in as many quantities as there were kinds and grades of all other goods and services in the market. No meaningful accounting system would be possible.

The second serious disadvantage of barter may be referred to as "the lack of a double coincidence of wants." [13] It would be a rare coincidence

[11] Einzig, *Primitive Money*, pp. 247–248; quoted in Ederer, *The Evolution of Money*, p. 30.
[12] Chandler, *Economics of Money and Banking*, p. 3.
[13] *Ibid.*

that the owner of a particular article which he wanted to trade would encounter another individual who wanted to trade and both wanted the other's commodity or service more than anything else in the market. Not only would each have to want the other's commodity more than any other, but both would need and have to be willing to trade quantities of approximate equal "use value" to the other.

A third major disadvantage to pure barter is the lack of a satisfactory unit of account in which to write contracts requiring payment in the future. Barter commodities vary in quality and grade; there would be little uniformity of goods or services, necessitating inspection of the commodity and a meeting of minds at the moment of trade. Under barter credit would be extremely difficult, making the development of loans and banking almost impossible.

Fourth, barter does not permit a sound method of storing generalized purchasing power. A stored commodity may deteriorate, storage may be costly, and the commodity may be difficult to dispose of without significant loss in value. Certain commodities could be stored more easily than others, making it easier for one man to store his wealth and impossible for another.

It is reasonable to state that barter in the broad sense has and does occur through all stages of history. But, because of the major shortcomings of barter, it is an extremely inefficient means of trade. "It was to overcome these difficulties that virtually every society invented some kind of money early in its development." [14]

2.3. Full-Bodied Money Systems

The origin of the history of Western civilization begins with the ancient societies of the Near East — Assyria, Babylonia, Persia, and Egypt. These agricultural societies flourished in the valleys of the Nile, Tigris, and Euphrates rivers around 4000 B.C. At this time these people developed the principles of metallurgy which opened the way to the widespread use of gold and silver.

The origin of money as we know it today had its roots in a cultural institution, namely in the communion meal of a sacrificial bull.[15] According to Desmonde, coins evolved in Greece and Rome from the ritualistic killing and eating of a divine bull. The bull was deified in most of the ancient Mediterranean cultures, including those of Egypt, Mesopotamia, Persia, Crete, and Greece as well as that of India. The central ritual in the Mithraic religion, which flourished throughout the Roman empire for centuries, was the sacrifice of a bull god.[16]

[14] *Ibid.*, p. 4.
[15] William H. Desmonde, *Magic, Myth, and Money: The Origin of Money in Religious Ritual* (New York: Free Press of Glencoe, 1962), p. 102.
[16] See Franz Cumont, *The Mysteries of Mithra* (Chicago: Open Court, 1910).

In the sacrificial ceremony a bull was led to a grating over a pit, and there he was killed with a sacred spear. The worshiper under the grate allowed his body to be drenched by the animal's blood. In this manner the worshiper was purified by the washing away of his sins. The testicles of the bull played an important role in the ceremony since the bull was frequently identified with fertility.

Not only was Dionysus often worshiped in the form of a bull but Homer frequently spoke of the offering of bulls. He spoke of the feast called the hekatomb, literally meaning one hundred oxen. Homer says of the sacrificial flesh that "each had his equal portion." [17] An inscription in Attica of around 330 B.C. contains a listing of the manner of distributing the bull's flesh:

Five pieces each to the presidents
Five pieces each to the nine archons
One piece each to the treasurers of the goddess
One piece each to the managers of the feast
The customary portions to others[18]

Through a process of "contagious magic" many of the objects connected with the ritual became imbued with varying degrees of holiness. Thus, the sacrifice became the source of certain religious souvenirs and relics, and these items were the immediate predecessors of ancient coinage.

Not only did the bull serve as a representative of a god, it also functioned as a standard of value.[19] According to Professor Bernhard Laum, the bull's significance as a standard of value arose from the sacrificial ritual in which the animal's flesh was divided by the communicants according to ancient standards of justice.

Most economists' theories neglect the psychological, cultural, and social setting of monetary symbols. However, these factors are of extreme importance to any analysis of innovation. Recent studies indicate that commerce as we know it was very likely an invention of the Greeks; Desmonde states that "Prior to this innovation, economic transactions were carried out along the lines of patriarchal redistribution, traditionally determined equivalences of interchange (as in kinship reciprocities), and through long-distance movements of goods based on values fixed by custom or state authority." [20]

[17] Desmonde, *Magic, Myth, and Money*, p. 104.
[18] Royden Keith Yerkes, *Sacrifice in Greek and Roman Religion* (Cambridge at the University Press, 1908), p. 481; referred to in Desmonde, *Magic, Myth, and Money*, pp. 104–105.
[19] Recall Kent's definition of money, "anything that is commonly used and generally accepted as a medium of exchange or as a standard of value." In this case the standard-of-value function came into existence prior to and exclusive of a common medium of exchange.
[20] Desmonde, *Magic, Myth, and Money*, p. 111.

Similar to the reciprocities among individuals, according to Laum, was the sacrifice to the gods, an exchange with the deities.[21] Offerings were made to the gods with the expectation of receiving specific benefits such as a good harvest or protection against illness. In ancient Greece offerings were not rigidly fixed; however, in early Rome specific concessions from the gods were thought obtainable for a definitely prescribed sacrificial dedication. According to Desmonde, the sacrificial ceremony later evolved into a regular exchange controlled and governed by the priests in accordance with religious laws. He gives the following example:

As in *Leviticus,* the animal which was brought to the god had to conform to painstakingly described rules; otherwise the ritual was of no avail. The offering was thus of a very definite type and character, a valuable good of rigidly determined quality. Insofar as atonement was the object of the votary, this good served as a fixed unit of absolution or propitiation: in a legal sense it functioned as a payment in an exchange between god and man.[22]

Thus, the religious ritual established a rigidly described medium of exchange and a good of guaranteed economic value. Because the bull served as the standard of value, when metals were introduced into the Greco-Roman society, their values were reckoned in terms of the sacred animal.

Imitations of animals were formed out of metal and were used in ancient ceremonies. In some cases artificial animal miniatures were offered in the place of actual animals; their purpose was also to serve as a means of payment and atonement to the gods. According to Laum these objects were manufactured by the temple establishments and were obtained by worshipers for purposes of offerings in exchange for other goods. Because of their use in offerings, these ornaments became units of value. Metallic formations were shaped to represent many of the objects used in the sacrificial ceremony — bull heads, pots, tripods, the spit. For example, the spit on which the animal was roasted was called *obelos.* In the course of time small ornaments representing the obelos circulated as money and later became the well-known Greek coin, the *obolos.*

"The first coins were produced from an abundant natural alloy of gold and silver called 'electrum,' and most numismatists accept Herodotus' statement that the Lydians in Asia Minor were the first to engage in minting." [23] Oftentimes it is explained that precious metals were chosen as money because to be used effectively money must be

[21] *Ibid.,* p. 114. Desmonde cites Bernhard Laum, *Heiliges Geld* (Tubingen: J. C. B. Mohr, 1924).
[22] *Ibid.,* p. 112.
[23] *Ibid.,* p. 112.

scarce, durable, portable, homogeneous, divisible, and readily identi-
fiable. However, many precious metals possessed qualities other than
these which may help to explain their use as money.

Certain types of stones were attributed different degrees of magical
potency by ancient man. "The employment of precious stones in
antiquity for the decoration of images of the deities and in religious
ceremonies, particularly funeral rites, stemmed from the belief in their
wondrous mystical virtues." [24] Gold, according to G. Elliot Smith, was
used for ornamental purposes because of the magical qualities attributed
to it by the ancient Egyptians.[25] Most of the precious metals existed
"in a mystic sympathy with an astral body, which exerted an influence
upon its properties . . . Gold had astrological affinity with the sun,
silver the moon, iron with Mars, quicksilver with Mercury, tin with
Jupiter, copper with Venus, and lead with Saturn." [26]

Gold has served as a medium of exchange for thousands of years,
and in many early cultures it was associated with the sun. In Egypt
the sun god in Crete took the form of a bull, and the moon goddess
took the shape of a cow.[27] Gold has also been associated with kingship
and royalty, and since the earliest times gold has been regarded as a
"noble" metal to be distinguished from "base" metals.

It is generally accepted that gold was used as a means of payment in
bullion form prior to the invention of minting around the seventh
century B.C. in Lydia. By the time of Croesus, coinage in Lydia was
under the control of the king; however, prior to that time monetary
historians differ as to whether the issuing agents were originally private
individuals, such as bankers or state authorities. Nevertheless, it seems
clear that many mystical, religious, and cultural influences played a
large role in the evolution of exchange from barter to full-bodied
money.

2.4. Representative and Credit Money Systems

Soon after the invention of coinage the guarantee of the state as to
fineness and weight of the Lydian stater caused the coin's total value to
exceed the value of its metallic content. Over time monarchs discovered
they could take advantage of this agio, and they began to appropriate
part of the metal as the payment for certification, i.e., as seigniorage.

2.4.1. State-Issued Representative and Credit Money. Following the
Lydian inauguration of coinage, it would be reasonable to assume that

[24] *Ibid.*, p. 122. Reference is made to George Frederick Kunz, *The Curious Lore of Precious Stones* (Philadelphia: Lippincott, 1913), p. 225.
[25] G. Elliot Smith, *The Ancient Egyptians* (London: Harper, 1923), p. 213.
[26] Desmonde, *Magic, Myth, and Money*, p. 122.
[27] Jane E. Harrison, *Themis* (Cambridge at the University Press, 1927).

the states closest to Lydia soon minted coins of their own. Coinage probably spread to other cities of Asia Minor and from there to continental Greece. Because of the supremacy of Athens, history witnessed the first appearance of a coin favored for international trade. The drachma soon became the most widely accepted and sought-after monetary unit for years.

The Athenians possessed large amounts of silver, which were primarily used instead of electrum for coinage. Historians speculate that the drachma originated in Aegina, and its value was equal to a handful of oboli, which were shaped like small spits or rods. The value of the drachma (six silver oboli) remained constant until the time of Solon's reform in 594 B.C. The reform of the monetary system of Athens appeared as follows:

```
 6 oboli     = 1 drachma
20 drachmas = 1 stater
 5 staters   = 1 mina
60 mina      = 1 talent[28]
```

From Solon's debasement of the drachma to the equivalent of 67 grains of silver, Alexander caused its further debasement to 65 grains, at which valuation it remained until the Roman conquest. Even during the Roman Empire, the drachma was more generally accepted than the Roman denarius, which was patterned after the Greek drachma.

The Roman denarius first appeared in 268 B.C. and contained about 66 grains of silver, like the Greek coin. Even though the value of the denarius remained relatively constant, the copper coins used prior to the denarius were continually debased. It was not until about 87 B.C. that the first gold coins were minted by the Romans. It was under Augustus that the gold coin, the aureus, was made an official coin of the empire valued at 25 denarii. Until the fall of the Roman Empire, its monetary system was as follows:

```
1 aureus    = 25 denarii
1 denarius = 4 sestercii
1 sestercius = 4 aera[29]
```

When Hannibal threatened Rome in 216 B.C. the denarius was reduced in weight from one-sixth to one-seventh of an ounce. Under Nero the Roman coins were continually debased.

When Nero had finished with the denarius, it contained up to 10% alloy. He had likewise decreased the size of the gold aureus so that there were forty-five to the libra instead of forty. Succeeding emperors all took a turn debasing the coinage. Under Trajan, the alloy in the denarius was increased to 25%, and when the spiral was brought to

[28] Ederer, *Evolution of Money*, p. 86.
[29] *Ibid.*, p. 88.

a halt, too late, in 300 A.D. by Diocletian, the denarius was practically a copper coin being only slightly washed with silver. The best coins had about 5% silver.[30]

Due to the limitation of their issue and the certification of the state, token coins generally circulate at a monetary value above the value of the materials of which they are made. In ancient Athens the monetary unit evolved relatively quickly from a full-bodied money to a credit money, completely bypassing a stage of full-bodied representative money. By A.D. 300 public confidence in the monetary system had waned appreciably, and the Romans began to return to more primitive exchange systems. Coins were weighed, tested, and eventually given up altogether in favor of barter. The barter system was facilitated somewhat by the fact that the old monetary unit continued to serve as a standard of value.

In Western Europe exchange for the most part was carried on through barter until the florin was introduced by Florence in A.D. 1252.[31] The reintroduction of coinage to Western Europe and its wide acceptance soon made Florence a prosperous banking center. According to Ederer, "The florins were good coins having about fifty-four grains of fine gold." He estimates that by A.D. 1300 there were over two million florins issued, and it became the international money of the day. Soon Genoa issued the Genoviva (or ducat) in A.D. 1284, and by 1350 nearly every significant sovereign in Western Europe had undertaken to issue coins patterned after the florin.[32]

Before turning attention to bank-issued money as the next stage of monetary evolution, it would be helpful to consider some of the experiments with state-issued paper money. Ederer concludes that the first state-issued paper money appeared in China as early as the ninth century A.D.[33] These paper notes were completely representative having as their backing 100 percent in metallic coins. It took little time, however, for the state to realize the agio, and it began to issue unbacked money and eventually irredeemable paper currency. Specie was restored for the most part during the reign of the first emperor of the Ming dynasty, around the latter part of the fourteenth century. Paper money again reappeared and became the most extensively used medium of exchange in China and the entire civilized world by the eighteenth and ninteenth centuries.

2.4.2. Bank-Issued Representative and Credit Money. In many Western

[30] *Ibid.*
[31] Arthur R. Burns, *Money and Monetary Policy in Early Times* (New York: Knopf, 1927), p. 53.
[32] Ederer, *Evolution of Money*, p. 90.
[33] *Ibid.*, p. 91.

European countries in the early seventeenth century, conditions existed that led to the private insurance of payment media. In 1609, the Bank of Amsterdam was organized to give the community relief from worn and defaced coins. One function of the bank was to accept for safekeeping in perpetuity gold and silver coins and to make credit transfers from one account to another on written orders.[34]

Coins were deposited with the bank at a discount of 5 percent, and the depositor was charged a service fee of ten florins to cover the costs of opening his account. The accounts were not convertible into specie; however, they could be sold to others. Brokers were employed by the bank to purchase the written orders offered. According to the organization plans for the bank, it was to keep all gold and silver received as a 100 percent reserve against deposits.

In 1790, one hundred and eighty years after the bank was opened, it was discovered that a large part of the gold and silver reserves had been lent illegally to the city government, the provinces of Holland, and the East India Company. Public confidence was lost, and the bank failed even though it had operated under the guaranty of the city. It is not known for exactly how long this bank operated successfully on what amounted to a fractional reserve deposit system.

The evolution of many money and banking practices in the United States had their origin in the development of payment media systems in Great Britain. Accordingly the remainder of this section primarily will be devoted to the origin of exchange systems in Great Britain.

In England during the early part of the seventeenth century, many merchants established the practice of depositing their gold in the Tower of London for safekeeping. In the early 1640s Charles I, who had become desperately in need of funds, unknowingly to the merchants seized most of the gold for his own use. As a result the merchants sought safekeeping elsewhere and began to make deposits of money with goldsmiths and money changers. The goldsmith issued his customers "goldsmith notes." These simple receipts were written promises to pay the customer, or to his order, a certain sum of money. In all probability money transfers first were made orally. An individual would visit the goldsmith or money changer and instruct him to transfer money to a payee. Thus, giro payments came into widespread use. Written orders began to be used as a means of directing the goldsmith to pay a certain person or to that person's order to the bearer of the note. These orders to pay differed from modern checks only in being less uniform.

[34] Some historians claim that the "check" was invented by the Romans as early as 352 B.C.

The initiative of some of the more enterprising money changers led them to begin taking the liberty of investing a portion of the deposits left with them for safekeeping. The evidence points to the overdraft as being the first widespread form of 100 percent reserve violation. The practice spread rapidly. It appears that the departure from the 100 percent reserve principle may have been the most radical and influential innovation in the history of monetary evolution to date.

The oldest bank in England, the Bank of England, was established in 1694.[35] It was organized under the reign of William and Mary under a contract requiring it to lend all its original capital to the government. Bank notes were issued in an amount equal to the bank's capital. Today, the Bank of England has a monopoly of note issue in England and Wales. Originally the bank was private; however, in 1946 it was nationalized by the Labour government.

After the turn of the eighteenth century, when other banks were established in London, people began to use banks as the primary institutions for depositing their money, and by the latter 1700s the use of checks for settling debts and transferring funds became commonplace. It was during the latter half of the eighteenth century that the word "check" first came to be used. Soon people receiving checks drawn on different banks found it inconvenient to go to the various banks to receive payment. They began depositing checks in their own banks, which did the collecting by presenting checks to the other banks with the use of messengers. Each bank's messenger found it necessary to make many trips every day to every other bank.

According to a well-known old story one day a weary messenger stopped at a coffeehouse, and as he drank his coffee he noticed another bank messenger with his bundle of checks. As it turned out, each carried a bundle of checks drawn on the other's bank; they decided to exchange checks and return to their own banks. Soon many messengers, learning of this simple method, started meeting at the coffeehouse; they all exchanged checks and returned to their respective banks. As time went on, the bankers realized the value of this system, and today the local "clearing house" plays an integral part in the system of check clearing and collection.

[35] It is generally accepted today that the first public bank was the municipal Bank of Barcelona, established in 1401. A similar deposit bank was founded in Genoa in 1407, the Casa di San Georgio. The bank most often referred to, however, as the real origin of modern commercial banking is the Banco della Piazza del Rialto established in Venice in 1584 (later called the Bank of Venice). The example of Venice was soon followed elsewhere: the Bank of Amsterdam was established in 1609, the Bank of Hamburg in 1619, the Bank of Stockholm in 1688, the Bank of England in 1694, and the Bank of Vienna in 1703.

After 1750 there was a rapid growth in country banking in England; before this time, British banking was almost entirely confined to London. As the use of banks became more widespread, considerable attention was focused on the effects of the banking and monetary system on general economic activity. Many noted scholars during the latter half of the eighteenth century concerned themselves with the operations and economic implications of the growth of the English banking system. According to Mints, the early ideas expressed during this period in the writings of Richard Cantillon, David Hume, Adam Dickson, and Adam Smith laid a foundation and the broad outlines from which a large part of banking theory was later drawn.[36]

During the latter part of the 1700s, banking began in the United States. In 1781, the Bank of North America was chartered and was the first institution in the United States to receive deposits, make loans, and issue notes.[37] The Bank operated in the city of Philadelphia, the political and financial capital at that time. Within a few years after the opening of the Bank of North America, New York, Massachusetts, and other states followed the example of Pennsylvania by making provisions for state-chartered banks. Within ten years, there were fourteen banks having an average capitalization of one million dollars. The development of banking and payment-media systems of the United States will be treated in considerable detail in Chapter 3.

Close to the turn of the nineteenth century, Great Britain experienced a wave of financial disturbances, and the Bank of England restricted cash payments from 1797 to 1821. The report of the Bullion Committee in 1810, and to a less extent the Report of the Committee on Irish Exchange in 1804, were responsible for a great increase in public concern and writings on monetary and banking theory. The monopoly position of the Bank of England was attacked, and there developed some resistance to the renewal of the Bank's charter. Controversies between the writers during this period led to a division of thought into two fairly coherent groups, which have been referred to as the "currency school" and the "banking school." [38]

Since 1844 the Bank of England has had two major departments, the note issue department and the banking department. The note issue department continued the issuance of Bank of England notes, and it is responsible for holding government securities, gold bullion, and coins which are pledged as collateral. The separation of the note-issue department from the banking department was done to justify the practice of

[36] Lloyd W. Mints, *A History of Banking Theory in Great Britain and the United States* (Chicago: University of Chicago Press, 1945), pp. 21–27.
[37] *Ibid.*, p. 61.
[38] See Mints, *History of Banking Theory*, pp. 74–124.

computing the reserves of the banking department in terms of Bank of England notes.

During the Great Depression in the early 1930s, there was an extensive overhauling of both the United States' and Great Britain's monetary systems. In 1931 England departed from a convertible gold standard. Bank notes now are treated by the banking department as an asset which it uses to meet its obligations. The same Bank of England notes are used by the commercial banks for the identical purpose. The Exchange Equalisation Account was established in 1931 to steady the external value of the pound sterling, and minor measures were adopted for regulating foreign borrowing. As was the case in the United States during this time period, bank and monetary legislation was concerned primarily with promoting financial and economic stability. The responsibility for monetary policy naturally moved to the government in 1946, when the Bank of England passed into public ownership.

The British banking system has undergone little change even with the stresses of World War II and the postwar economic developments. "The banks, enjoying complete public confidence, function through a closely coordinated system, and for well over half a century checks drawn on them have constituted the principal means of settlement and remittance." [39] Structural simplification of the banking system has been achieved through the incorporation, during the past century, of local, country banks into a few institutions. Among the principal banks in England are the "Big Five," all with countrywide branch systems. These five banks, Barclays, Lloyds, Midland, National Provincial, and Westminister, constitute approximately three-quarters of the banking resources of the United Kingdom.

Further coordination of the English banking system presently is being achieved by the implementation of vast on-line computer networks.[40] In mid-1967, three of the "Big Five" announced plans to link their respective head offices and branches throughout the country. Barclays, with $6.4 billion in deposits and 2,500 branch offices, is acquiring a Burroughs B8500 computer system and 2,300 terminal computers. The order is believed to be the largest ever placed for an information-processing system by a private firm. Midland Bank and Westminister Bank will operate together 2,650 terminal units valued in excess of $20 million. Delivery of the systems is scheduled for 1969 and 1970. The two major reasons for the institutions' entry into on-line banking are given as (1) decimalization of the British currency,

[39] Benjamin Haggott Beckhart, Banking Systems (New York: Columbia University Press, 1954), p. 779.
[40] See "British Banks Plan Vast On-Line Networks," Burroughs Clearing House, May 1967, p. 78.

scheduled for 1970, which will entail the conversion of thousands of business machines to the decimal system; and (2) the proposed establishment of a computerized postal giro system for effecting payments without checks, which will compete with banks for small as well as big customers' accounts.[41]

Another recent development in British banking has been the introduction of the bank credit card. In 1966, Barclays began issuing credit cards, announcing that the bank hoped soon to obtain one million cardholders with an annual monetary turnover of 100 million pounds. Within weeks, the Midland Bank began to issue "cheque cards," which serve as a limited guarantee of customers' check credit. Midland officials did not attempt to disguise the fact that their "cheque card" plan was designed with the intention of "defeating" the Barclays credit-card system.[42] Of these two latest innovations in the British payment media system, one appears to promise increased cooperation and coordination while the other has opened new avenues for increased competition.

[41] *Ibid.* A giro credit transfer system is a financial system in which credit circulation takes the place of checks, banknotes, and coins. Most of the Western European countries operate giro systems, of which there are two basic kinds: postal giro systems (a public system operated through a country's post offices) and bank giro systems (a private system operated through a country's commercial banking system). For a more complete description of giro credit-transfer systems, see Appendix I. Also see F. P. Thomson, *Giro Credit Transfer Systems* (Oxford: Pergamon Press, 1964).

[42] See, "This Could Mean Banking War," *The Economist,* January 15, 1966, p. 220, and "Credit Cards—Midland's Model Army," *The Economist,* January 22, 1966.

**The History
of Payment
Media Systems
in the
United States**

Chapter Three

The history of payment media systems in the United States depicts an evolution through the three stages in the development of exchange media even though the use of barter, full-bodied money, and representative and credit money can all still be found today. Generally speaking, however, it is possible to trace the evolution of payment media in the United States through successive stages of development as one stage became the predominant system and a former system was gradually replaced. This chapter will discuss the historical evolution of exchange in the United States and set the foundation for an analysis of our present system of payment media, which is presented in Chapter 4.

Although many societies may be operating under similar exchange systems, each one will have developed a financial system that is best suited to its own needs and that is therefore in many respects unique. It is important therefore when attempting to chart the future development of payment media in a particular society to consider the influence of that society's requirements in the innovative process. Naturally, the development of the United States' banking system represents the single most important institutional framework surrounding the evolution of payment media systems in the United States. Accordingly, considerable attention is devoted to the history and development of American banking practices and institutions.

During the relatively brief history of the United States there has been an extensive degree of experimentation with payment media systems. Basically the monetary standards under which this country has operated have not been new phenomena; they have been utilized elsewhere in the world. It was stressed earlier, however, that the process of innovation must include the implementation of a phenomenon in such a way as to achieve the goals of society. Oftentimes a new development will be experimented with and rejected by a society only to be accepted at a later time. This process of experimentation, gradual assimilation, or rejection deserves attention; it should provide some insights into society's reaction to future developments.

The historical evolution of payment media systems in the United

States can be divided into six periods: (1) early colonial exchange systems; (2) bimetallism, 1792–1862; (3) fiat money, 1862–1879; (4) the gold coin standard, 1873–1933; (5) the managed gold standard, 1933–1968; (6) fiat money, March 18, 1968, to the present.

3.1. Early Colonial Exchange Systems

During the early history of the American colonies, barter was a major system of exchange.[1] Basic necessities were traded among small groups of settlers. Certain commodities began to be used as the principal media of exchange: corn, tobacco, beads, pelts, and gunpowder. The colonists were familiar with English coins; however, under British rule they were not allowed a national coinage. Consequently the coins which were used were ones which happened to reach them in the course of trade. This led to considerable confusion because the trade relationship between the colonies and the rest of the world brought into domestic circulation coins from many different countries, including the Spanish dollar and its subdivisions; the British pounds, shillings, and pence; the French guinea and pistole; and the Portuguese moidore and johannes.[2]

As trade developed, more reliance was placed on the use of foreign coins as media of exchange. Because of the nature of our trade relationships with other countries, the Spanish dollar and its subdivisions constituted the major exchange medium.[3] Most of the British coins were exported to pay for goods. The most important export market for the colonies was the West Indies, with whom the colonies maintained a favorable balance of trade. The result was a relatively large inflow of Spanish dollars. Some of these coins were used to finance the unfavorable balance of trade with Britain; the remainder passed into general circulation. During much of this period, financial records were kept in pounds, shillings, and pence. This is an example of a society in which one monetary unit served as a unit of account and another served as the primary medium of exchange.

In this early period, there was a shortage of money. Massachusetts tried to meet the need for metallic money by the coinage of the "pine tree" shilling, but the mint was later closed by the British.[4] Resort was also made to the issuance of fiat money in the form of "bills of credit"

---

[1] See Arthur Nussbaum, *A History of the Dollar* (New York: Columbia University Press, 1957), Chapter 1.

[2] Barton Hepburn, *History of Coinage in the United States* (New York: Macmillan, 1930), pp. 11–13.

[3] See D. R. Dewey, *Financial History of the United States* (New York: Longmans, Green, 1928), 10th ed., pp. 18–21.

[4] The Massachusetts mint, which was established in 1652 and closed in 1688, also minted a limited number of three-penny and six-penny coins.

and "loan bills"; however, these bills were issued to such an excess that they quickly depreciated.

The Revolutionary War and its attendant expenses forced the Second Continental Congress to issue paper money supposedly redeemable in specie; in fact the notes were irredeemable paper money.[5] The money depreciated sharply in value as the hope of redemption eventually vanished. By 1781, the notes ceased to circulate as money. When the paper currency was circulating, most of the four million dollars in coins in the colonies was hoarded.

Because of the shortage of money, several states permitted the issuance of private coins. Competition among private sources led to debasement and overissuance. Gresham's law led to financial difficulties which help to explain the provision in the United States Constitution giving Congress the exclusive power "to coin money, regulate the value thereof, and of foreign coins. . . ." [6]

3.2. Bimetallism, 1792–1862

Bimetallism was established by the Coinage Act of 1792. The Act provided for a United States Mint, "full-bodied" gold and silver coins, token copper coins, and the free coinage of gold and silver coins. The silver dollar was to consist of 371.25 grains of fine silver, and the gold dollar to consist of 24.75 grains of fine gold. The mint ratio of silver to gold was 15 to 1; this ratio undervalued gold, which tended to disappear from the United States. In 1834, an attempt was made to correct the mint ratio, and the gold dollar was redefined to consist of 23.2 grains, making the new ratio 16:1. However, silver was then undervalued, and the result was a disappearance of silver money from the currency system.

Since the colonists thought of banking primarily as a source of paper money, nearly all banks during this period were banks of issue. Prior to 1838, the chartering of a bank required the approval of Congress or the state legislature where the bank was to be located. Obtaining a charter was difficult because of the poor attitude which existed toward banks. In the words of James Guthrie, "As late as 1853 the Secretary of the Treasury expressed the hope that the increase in the supply of the precious metals in this country (following gold discovery in Cali-

---

[5] Habits and tradition are important influencing factors in monetary affairs. When a monetary unit was formally adopted in the United States, the dollar was chosen over the pound simply because the Spanish dollar came into existence as the primary medium of exchange. In 1775 when the Second Continental Congress issued notes equivalent to 2,000,000 Spanish milled dollars and "payable" in dollars, it was the first official recognition of the dollar. Later the Coinage Act of 1792, officially designated the dollar as the money of account of the United States.

[6] *The Constitution of the United States*, Article 1, Section 8.

fornia) would continue a few years longer so that we might yet find it possible to abolish banks and return to a purely metallic currency." [7]

Because these were banks of issue (technically, bank notes and specie were interchangeable) the continued success of a bank depended on its ability to keep its notes in circulation. Abuses occurred during this period when some banks ruthlessly exploited this concept by locating in the wilderness to prevent notes from being returned. This practice was referred to as "wildcat banking." It is difficult to assess the contribution during this period to the development of modern-day commercial banking; however, Bagehot attempts to justify the note issuing privilege by insisting that no nation has ever developed a great system of deposit banking without first going through this preliminary stage.[8]

The first bank of the United States was chartered in 1791, for a twenty-year period. This bank was headquartered in Philadelphia and operated branches in the major cities in the country. It issued paper money redeemable in gold and silver which circulated throughout the country. "The aim of the bank's organizers was to establish a commercial bank to serve as a fiscal agent for the government, a source of loanable funds, a bank of issue, and a bank of discount, combining the activities of a central bank and a commercial bank." [9] According to available sources the bank maintained a satisfactory relationship with the government, performed its functions well, and had a powerful following among many of the country's leaders. Nevertheless, its federal charter was permitted to lapse in 1811 — one year before the War of 1812, when its services could have been put to great advantage.

The aftermath of the war found the United States in considerable financial difficulty. Specie payments were suspended by the banks, and they disappeared from circulation. Prices during a four-year period doubled, and Congress chartered the Second Bank of the United States in 1816. The intended functions of this bank were identical with those of the first bank. Initially the bank's operations were reckless under its first president, William Jones. Under the second and third presidents, Langdon Cheves and Nicholas Biddle, however, the bank's operations became sound. In 1831, Congress passed a bill providing for the rechartering of the bank, but the bill was vetoed by President Andrew Jackson.

---

[7] James Guthrie, *Finance Reports* (1853), p. 10; Cf. Message of the Governor of Michigan (January 2, 1843), in United States House of Representatives, 29th Cong., 1st sess., Doc. 226, p. 1215 (quoted), quoted in Charles L. Prather, *Money and Banking*, 8th ed. (Homewood, Ill.: Irwin, 1965), p. 122.

[8] See Walter Bagehot, *Lombard Street* (London: John Murray, 1915), 14th ed., p. 88.

[9] Prather, *Money and Banking*, p. 126.

State banking flourished during this period, and when the First and Second Banks of the United States were no longer present to exercise a restraining influence on unwise banking practices, such practices also flourished. Many of the abuses were associated with the issuance of bank paper money, and several developments occurred in an attempt to curtail these practices.

The Suffolk Banking System, which started in Boston in 1824, was notably successful. If out-of-town banks would keep specie available at the Suffolk Bank in Boston to assure that their notes could be redeemed, they would not be prodded. If a bank refused to cooperate, the banks participating in the system would persistently send its notes for redemption in specie. By 1825, virtually all New England banks were part of the system, which maintained circulation of its notes at par. The system emphasized the principle of convertibility not only at the bank of issue but also at a central redemption center. This same principle is applicable to checks and today represents a major function of the Federal Reserve System.

The problems surrounding the issuance of bank notes grew substantially in most parts of the country with few exceptions. Louisiana was an exception. Among other things the Louisiana Bank Act of 1842 provided strict regulations on the reserves supporting bank notes. Reserves were to consist of one-third specie and two-thirds short-term commercial paper. The Act remained in effect until the Civil War reconstruction period and became the forerunner of the fractional reserve system for deposits.

Under the Safety Fund System organized in New York in 1829, each bank was required to contribute 3 percent of its capital stock to a guaranty fund. The fund was used for discharging the liabilities of insolvent banks. The system operated successfully until the panic of 1837, when there was an insufficient amount of money to meet all the losses. Even though the original arrangement of the Safety Fund was amended in 1845, the principle was sound, and this same concept was applied in 1933, when Congress provided for deposit insurance by a federal agency, The Federal Deposit Insurance Corporation.

The panic of 1837 brought with it much public condemnation of banking. Starting with New York several states passed "free-banking" legislation, which provided for the chartering of new banks without a special act of the legislature. During the period from 1834 to 1861, the number of banks increased from five hundred to sixteen hundred; the increase was mostly in the fourteen states which passed "free-banking" laws.

During the same period there were two other important developments in banking practices. The large growth of the number of banks led to the development of correspondent relations among many banking houses, particularly in New York. At about the same time the growth in the value and volume of checks led the New York banks to organize the New York Clearinghouse in 1854. Soon after, clearinghouses were organized in most of the other major financial centers.

3.3. Fiat Money, 1862–1879

With the outbreak of the Civil War gold payments were suspended immediately by the banks, and Congress authorized three issues of United States notes totaling $450 million.[10] The large amount of notes and the general lack of confidence in their ultimate redeemability led people to hoard gold. The paper money depreciated in value, and prices increased to more than double their 1861 level.[11] During this entire period, "From 1862 to 1879, there was no official link between the U.S. dollar and gold. . . ." [12]

A development of considerable importance in the decade 1860–1870 was the passage of the National Currency Act in 1863 and the establishment of the national banking system. There were two main objectives of this legislation: (1) to improve the quality of the country's currency and the banking system, and (2) to help sell government bonds. National banks were required to keep reserves against deposit liabilities — 25 percent for banks in cities designated as "central reserve" or "reserve," and 15 percent in other cities. Two years later, Congress levied a 10 percent tax on the note issues of state banks, which for all practical purposes denied them the note-issue privilege. Within several years' time the number of state banks declined drastically while the number of national banks increased over threefold. The shift of state banks into the national banking system brought most banks in the country under the supervision of the Comptroller of the Currency.

The major advantage of the legislation of 1863–1864 was the maintenance of a sound monetary unit. The national bank notes as a medium of exchange circulated at par regardless of the issuing bank, and the holders of these notes did not suffer a loss if a bank failed. A major source of recurring difficulties, however, was the lack of elasticity of the currency supply.

In 1873, a bill was passed by Congress which eliminated the standard

[10] These notes originally were not redeemable in gold, and they were popularly referred to as "greenbacks."

[11] See E. M. Lerner, "Inflation in the Confederacy, 1861–1865," in Milton Friedman, ed., *Studies in the Quantity Theory of Money* (Chicago: University of Chicago Press, 1956), pp. 163–175.

[12] Milton Friedman and Anna J. Schwartz, *A Monetary History of the United States, 1867–1960* (Princeton: Princeton University Press for the National Bureau of Economic Research, 1963), p. 85.

silver dollar as an official United States coin. At the time, this provision had little practical significance;[13] however, it officially ended legal bimetallism and made the gold dollar the standard unit of value. In 1878, pressure on Congress led to the passage of the Bland-Allison Act, which required the Secretary of the Treasury to purchase from two to four million dollars of silver per month at the current market price. The silver was used for the coinage of standard silver dollars and as a basis for the issuance of silver certificates.[14]

3.4. Gold Coin Standard, 1879–1933[15]

The Specie Resumption Act in 1875 called for the redemption of greenbacks in gold beginning in 1879, putting the United States on a gold coin standard. Purchases of silver by the Treasury were increased in 1890 with the passage of the Sherman Silver Purchase Act. The Bland-Allison Act was repealed, and the Treasury was directed to buy as much as 4,500,000 ounces of silver a month. The silver was to be purchased with new silver certificates which were made legal tender.[16]

During the decade of the 1890s it became difficult to maintain gold redemption. The increased flow of silver certificates into the monetary system together with disturbed economic conditions caused people to exchange much of their paper money for gold. Financial disturbances in Europe caused many foreign bankers to convert their United States investments into gold. Adverse economic conditions reached their culmination in the panic of 1893, and during the following depressionary period the excessive demand for gold nearly caused the United States to suspend gold redemption. The situation was relieved somewhat with the repeal of the Sherman Silver Purchase Act in 1893, but it was necessary for the government to sell $262 million of bonds by 1896 in order to purchase gold for redemption purposes. Confidence in the country's monetary system returned after the presidential campaign of 1896.

[13] Because the country was on a paper standard, little attention was given to the official elimination of silver as a monetary standard. Prior to 1873, silver could be converted into coin at a fixed price of $1.29 per ounce; by 1879, the market price of silver dropped to $1.12. The discovery of rich silver mines in Nevada led to considerable opposition to the "Crime of '73" and pressure for return to bimetallism.

[14] The fact that this money was not redeemable in gold but treated as standard money to the extent that they were made unlimited legal tender, the monetary standard has been referred to as a "limping standard."

[15] The United States operated under a gold coin standard until 1933, except for a brief period when it was suspended shortly after entry into World War I. This suspension period was in effect from September 1917 to June 1919.

[16] The silver certificates, known as Treasury Notes of 1890, were made redeemable in either gold or silver at the option of the Secretary of the Treasury. A total of $155,931,000 of these certificates was issued before the repeal of the Sherman Act in 1893.

The legal position of the silver dollar was settled with the passage of the Gold Standard Act of 1900. The Act directed the Secretary of the Treasury to maintain all forms of money at par with gold. Most of the gold in the United States was held by the government and the banks; besides the silver certificates, the notes of 1890, and fractional coins, the public circulated gold certificates.

After the turn of the century monetary problems were essentially settled. There was an inflow of gold primarily from the Yukon and South Africa which permitted an expansion of the money supply.[17] With the passage of time, however, inadequacies of the banking system became apparent. Several major deficiencies were

1. The currency was not elastic. The national bank notes failed to contract and expand with the needs of the community.[18]

2. Bank reserve requirements represented a weakness in the system. Reserves were pyramided because banks were permitted to redeposit them with correspondent banks.[19] There was also a failure to distinguish between reserves for demand and time deposits, and there was an overconcentration of reserves in New York.

3. There was little coordination of the banking system, and there was an extremely poor mechanism for the clearing and collection of checks. Banks would charge a fee ("an exchange charge") on a check presented for payment on an out-of-town bank. In order to avoid the exchange charge a bank would send out-of-town checks to its correspondent bank instead of by the most direct route. The correspondent bank would send the check to its correspondent bank. For example: A check drawn on a North Birmingham, Alabama, bank and deposited in a Birmingham bank four miles away, traveled 4,500 miles and took 14 days to get to the bank on which it was drawn. The check went from Birmingham to Jacksonville, Florida, and then to Philadelphia to get to North Birmingham. When payment was refused it traveled the same route in reverse to get back to Birmingham.[20]

---

[17] Two exceptions were the money panics of 1903 and 1907. The more severe 1907 financial disturbance occurred when business activity began to flatten out and gold left the country. The decline in the money supply led several small New York banks to suspend payments and other banks and trust companies experienced heavy demands for gold. Many banks placed restrictions on payment of currency; the contraction subsided and the crisis passed in 1908.

[18] This reflection of the "real bills" doctrine was to play an influential role in the writing of the Federal Reserve Act.

[19] All banks except central reserve city banks could include their deposits in reserve city and central reserve city banks as part of their legal reserve requirement.

[20] *The Story of Checks* (New York: The Federal Reserve Bank of New York, 1962), 2nd ed., p. 8.

In 1908, Congress passed the Aldrich-Vreeland Act, which permitted banks to issue emergency currency under restricted conditions and provided for a National Monetary Commission. The Commission was to study the country's payment media system and banking system. The recommendations of the Commission led to the passage of the Federal Reserve Act establishing the Federal Reserve System on December 23, 1913. As expressed by its founders its original purposes, ". . . were to give the country an elastic currency, to provide facilities for discounting commercial paper, and to improve the supervision of banking." [21] The Federal Reserve was given the power to issue Federal Reserve bank notes (to replace national bank notes) and Federal Reserve notes.[22]

Shortly before the Federal Reserve System began operations, World War I created many unforeseen conditions. An increase in exports to Europe resulted in a large inflow of gold, and the total stock of money increased considerably. Due to the conditions of issuance the supply of currency other than gold and national bank notes, however, remained relatively stable.[23] Prices increased substantially throughout the world; in the United States prices increased between 40 and 50 percent from 1897 to 1917.[24]

When the United States declared war on Germany in April 1917, the government was obliged to float large public loans, and the first important policy of the Federal Reserve was to assist in the war financing. The method which was adopted was the establishment of a preferential rate on paper secured by government obligations when it was discounted by member banks with the Federal Reserve; the obligations

[21] Board of Governors, *The Federal Reserve System Purposes and Functions,* (Washington: Board of Governors of the Federal Reserve System, 1963), 5th ed., p. 1.
[22] Since Federal Reserve banknotes were to be issued exclusively for the replacement of national bank notes, only a very few of them were issued under the original Federal Reserve Act. The Pittman Act of April 23, 1918, however, authorized the retirement of $350,000,000 worth of silver certificates and their replacement with Federal Reserve bank notes. Great Britain needed a large quantity of silver for currency redemption in India, and the United States agreed to sell the silver to Britain at a dollar per ounce. Silver certificates were called in by the Federal Reserve and exchanged at the Treasury for Pittman certificates of indebtedness. The Pittman certificates in turn were used as security for the issuance of the Federal Reserve Bank notes.
[23] For further explanation and a comprehensive analysis of the money supply during this period, see Friedman and Schwartz, *Monetary History of the United States,* pp. 173–183.
[24] According to Friedman and Schwartz, "The price rise in the United States after 1897 was part of a worldwide movement. British wholesale prices, which may be taken as reasonably representative of prices in the rest of the western world linked together by a common monetary standard, rose by 26 per cent from 1897 to 1914 according to the Board of Trade index." See p. 135, Friedman and Schwartz reference the *Board of Trade Journal,* Jan. 13, 1921, p. 34.

were called "war paper." The rate level made it possible for member banks to finance public purchases of government securities on an installment basis, without cost to the purchasers for the accommodation. The rate paid to member banks on these securities was the coupon rate on the bonds. The banks then discounted the paper with the Federal Reserve at a lower rate, and the difference compensated the banks for carrying the accounts. The result was a great expansion of member-bank and Federal Reserve bank credit.

For more than a year after the end of the war, the Federal Reserve facilitated a continued increase in bank credit. The rediscount rate could have been raised, but the Treasury opposed any action which would have made more difficult the management of the public debt. From the beginning of United States' involvement in the war to mid-1920, there was a 25 percent increase in the money stock which accompanied a price inflation during this period.[25] In mid-1921 the Federal Reserve reversed its policy and induced monetary contraction; prices fell and business activity contracted sharply. The remainder of the decade of the 1920s was characterized by a large expansion of business activity.

Between the period 1921 and 1933, a most significant phenomenon was the large number of bank failures, indicated in Table 3.1. Around the beginning of the decade of the 1930s, the money supply began to shrink. As bank failures grew in number and importance, people converted deposits into currency. The demand for currency aggravated monetary contraction. During the early part of the Great Depression there was also an increase in foreign demand for gold, putting an additional downward pressure on the money stock. In 1933 over four thousand banks were suspended.[27]

3.5. Managed Gold Standard, 1933–1968 [28]

3.5.1. Developments Growing Out of the Great Depression. On the morning of March 6, 1933, President Franklin D. Roosevelt proclaimed a nationwide banking holiday. The Emergency Banking Act passed on March 9 gave the President sweeping authority over banking, currency, and foreign exchange. Under this authority President Roosevelt took

[25] See Friedman and Schwartz, *Monetary History of the United States,* Chapter 5.

[27] In 1932, two acts of Congress provided a small help in alleviating the crisis. The Reconstruction Finance Corporation was established with authority to support banks and provide financial assistance to state and local governments and to many private businesses. The Glass-Steagall Act granted the Federal Reserve more power and permitted the inclusion of government debt as well as commercial paper and gold as collateral for Federal Reserve notes.

[28] For a summary of United States' silver policies from 1933 to the present, see Appendix II.

Table 3.1. Commercial-Bank Suspensions in the United States, 1921–1932.

Year	National Banks	State Member Banks	State Nonmember Banks	All Banks	Total Deposits (thousands of dollars)
1921	52	19	434	505	172,188
1922	49	13	304	366	91,182
1923	90	32	524	646	149,601
1924	122	38	615	775	210,151
1925	118	28	472	618	167,555
1926	123	35	818	976	260,378
1927	91	31	547	669	199,329
1928	57	16	425	498	142,386
1929	64	17	578	659	230,643
1930	161	27	1,162	1,350	837,096
1931	409	107	1,777	2,293	1,690,232
1932	276	55	1,122	1,453	706,188

Source: *Federal Reserve Bulletin*, September 1937, pp. 868–873.

immediate action to nationalize all gold bullion and coin owned by the public; all persons were required to deliver to the Federal Reserve or to member banks all gold bullion, coin, and certificates on or before May 1, 1933. To strengthen the cash position of banks which suffered heavy withdrawals, authority was given for the issuance of new Federal Reserve bank notes.

The President was granted additional powers with the passage of the "Thomas Inflation Amendment" to the Agricultural Adjustment Act of May 12, 1933. The Act empowered him to reduce the weight of the gold dollar by as much as 50 percent; it also made all coins and currencies issued "by or under the authority of the United States" legal tender for the payment of all debts both public and private. Other provisions of the amendment were either not used or turned out to be of little significance. Another enactment of Congress was the Joint Resolution of June 5, 1933, which abrogated the gold clause in public and private contracts.[29]

The sound banks in the country were permitted to reopen; under authority of the Emergency Banking Act the President issued an execu-

[29] It had become the practice in long-term contracts to include a "gold clause" specifying payment in gold dollars of the standard of value existing at the time the contract was signed. This joint resolution removed any obligation to pay in gold that was previously made impossible by the nationalization of gold.

tive order on March 10 empowering the Secretary of the Treasury to license member banks to reopen. State banking authorities were also granted the right to permit the reopening of nonmember banks. By the end of March close to thirteen thousand banks were operating on an "unrestricted" basis.[30] In December jurisdiction over state non-member banks was returned to state authorities.

Fundamental reforms in the banking system were enacted on June 16, with the passage of the Banking Act of 1933. This comprehensive legislation primarily was designed to strengthen the banking system. Its main provisions were (1) the Federal Deposit Insurance Corporation was created to insure each bank account for $2,500; (2) the authority of national banks to establish branches was enlarged, and mutual savings banks and industrial savings banks were made eligible for admission to the Federal Reserve System; (3) investment interests were ordered divorced from commercial banks; (4) interest payments on demand deposits were forbidden and the Board of Governors was to fix interest rates on time deposits of member banks; (5) the capital requirement of new national banks established in communities of less than three thousand population was increased from twenty-five to fifty thousand dollars; (6) member banks were forbidden to make loans to their own executive officers; (7) the Federal Reserve Open Market Committee was established; (8) bank holding companies were required to obtain permits from the Federal Reserve Board in order to vote the stock of any member bank subsidiary, and permits would be granted only to those holding companies that permitted a certain degree of supervision and regulation of their activities; (9) the Federal Reserve Board was given the power to restrict the use of member bank credit for speculative purposes; and (10) the Federal Reserve Board was given jurisdiction over the international financial transactions of the Federal Reserve banks.

In the autumn of 1933, the Roosevelt administration undertook measures designed to increase prices to their 1926 level.[31] The price of gold was raised from $20.67 per fine ounce to $35.00, reducing the number of gold grains in each dollar from 25.8 to $15\frac{5}{21}$. Officially this change was made on January 31, 1934; however, the price level did not increase substantially for some time.

[30] *Federal Reserve Bulletin*, April 1933, p. 209.
[31] The objective in increasing prices was based on the monetary theories of Professor George F. Warren of Cornell University. Warren reasoned that the demand for gold had become so great relative to its short supply that the purchasing power of the dollar had increased, causing prices to decline. The remedy, he claimed, would be to devalue gold and increase prices.

On January 30, 1934, Congress passed the Gold Reserve Act — an enactment which had a profound impact on the United States monetary system. The Act provided that (1) the United States government take title to all gold bullion, coin, and certificates held by the Federal Reserve banks; (2) the Federal Reserve banks be compensated dollar for dollar at the old rate of $20.67 per ounce; (3) the Federal Reserve Act be amended in numerous places to substitute for "gold," "gold certificates," which were to constitute the reserves of the Federal Reserve banks; (4) the devaluation of the dollar be at least 60 percent of the dollar's pre-1934 rate even though the President could devalue the gold content of the dollar by 50 percent of its old rate; (5) two billion dollars of the profit of devaluation be appropriated to an Exchange Stabilization Fund for the purpose of controlling the value of the dollar in international exchange; (6) gold coins be melted down into gold bars and no currency of the United States be redeemable in gold.[32] This Act put the United States on a managed gold standard. The Gold Reserve Act together with the Banking Acts of 1933 and 1935, and the Bretton Woods Agreement Act of 1945, can be described as the basic monetary legislation as it stands in the United States at the present time.

The Banking Act of August 23, 1935, gave the Federal Reserve authorities greater power and scope, completing the reformation of the banking system begun in 1933. The September, 1935 *Federal Reserve Bulletin* describes this enactment in the following terms:

It incorporates into law much of the experience acquired by the System during the more than two decades of its operations. It reflects a broader conception of the System's functions in the country's economic life than existed at the time the System was established; it defines more clearly and fixes more firmly the responsibilities of the Board in Washington and the regional Reserve banks; it permanently removes from the operations of the Federal Reserve banks and the member banks some of the restrictions which at critical times prevent them from effectively rendering the services to the country for the performance of which they were established; and, finally, it clarifies and simplifies a number of features of the administration of the System.[33]

The major features of the Banking Act of 1935 can be summarized to include (1) the establishment of the "Board of Governors of the Federal Reserve System" to consist of seven men appointed for fourteen-year terms by the President with the advice and consent of the Senate.

---

[32] The provisions of the Gold Reserve Act declared the gold dollar to be the standard unit of value; however, since gold was to be melted down into bars this put the United States on a managed gold bullion standard.
[33] *Federal Reserve Bulletin,* September 1935, p. 559.

The Secretary of the Treasury and Comptroller of the Currency to be removed as ex-officio members of the Board; (2) vesting in the Board of Governors new powers including the authority to set reserve requirements within designated limits, to determine Federal Reserve bank discount rates and require changes more often than every two weeks, and to specify eligible paper for rediscounting to member banks; (3) reorganization of the Federal Reserve Open Market Committee to include the Board of Governors; vesting in the Federal Deposit Insurance Corporation new powers of regulation over nonmember state banks, and provision for increasing the insurance per account from $2,500 to $5,000; (4) elimination of the double liability on national bank stock issued prior to June 16, 1933; and (5) the expansion of national bank real-estate loan powers.

3.5.2. Developments from 1940 to the Present. There was a gradual improvement in economic conditions after the New Deal except for a setback in 1937, when a short recession intervened. Federal Reserve policy was again hampered by its efforts to support government obligations issued to help finance expenditures in World War II.[34] In part due to the huge increase in the federal debt[35] and a wartime decline in the monetary gold stock, Congress passed the Act of June 12, 1945, which reduced to 25 percent the gold-certificate reserve requirements applicable to the notes and deposit liabilities of the Federal Reserve Banks. At the same time, however, this enactment no

[34] Immediately after the outbreak of war on September 1, 1939, the Federal Reserve Open Market Committee met and decided to purchase freely in the open market in order to make clear the Federal Reserve's intent to support the government securities market. By the end of the war, the System's portfolio had increased tenfold.

The World War II period and its aftermath are particularly important to the study of the development of Federal Reserve monetary policy. Many changes occurred in the economy due to the financing of the war. The most conspicuous change was the fivefold growth of the Federal debt. By 1949, bank deposits were two and one half times as large as before the war, and money in the public's hands had grown by nearly 400 percent. The ensuing period of price inflation due in large measure to Federal Reserve purchases of government debt led to much Congressional debate over the conflict of interests between pegging security prices and enacting monetary policies toward economic stabilization. Recommendations made by the Subcommittee on Monetary, Credit, and Fiscal Policies of the Joint Committee on the Economic Report (headed by Senator Paul Douglas of Illinois) and concern expressed by President Truman led to the issuance of the famous "Accord" of March 4, 1951. This agreement between the United States Treasury and the Federal Reserve System meant that for the first time since 1935, the System was free to use monetary policies to achieve the objectives customarily assigned to a central bank.

[35] See H. C. Murphy, *The National Debt in War and Transition* (New York: McGraw-Hill, 1950).

longer allowed "lawful money" to serve as reserves against System deposit liabilities.

The Federal Reserve's authority to issue Federal Reserve bank notes was revoked with the passage of the Act of June 12, 1945. This legislation also revoked the authority of the President and the Secretary of the Treasury to issue United States notes under the terms of the Thomas Inflation Amendment of the Agricultural Adjustment Act of 1933. Since neither Federal Reserve bank notes nor United States notes were backed by gold reserves, their elimination by Congress seemed to indicate a Congressional emphasis on the gold standard.

In July 1944, representatives of forty-four countries met at Bretton Woods, New Hampshire, and approved the Articles of Agreement for the International Monetary Fund and the Articles of Agreement for the International Bank for Reconstruction and Development. The actions of these representatives were not binding on their governments; however, the United States was the first country to take action on the agreements by passage of the Bretton Woods Agreements Act on July 31, 1945.[36]

In addition to the establishment of two new international financial institutions, the purposes of the "Bretton Woods Agreements" were (1) modification of the gold values of currencies and promotion of exchange stability and equilibrium in international balance of payments; (2) elimination of foreign-exchange restrictions that curtail the growth of international trade; and (3) provision for a common pool of gold standard monies which could serve as media of exchange between nations and correct temporary maladjustments in a country's balance of payments.

Upon becoming a member of the International Monetary Fund, the United States indicated again that the "par value" of the dollar would be 15$\frac{5}{21}$ grains of gold 9/10 fine, the same value which was proclaimed under the Gold Reserve Act of 1934. The United States' original subscription to the Fund was $2,750 million, of which $687.5 million was payable in gold and the remainder in United States dollars. Most of the funds were provided from the assets of the Treasury's Exchange Stabilization Fund. Congress permitted the Stabilization Fund to continue operations even though its two billion dollars in assets (as provided for by the Gold Reserve Act) had been reduced to a mere two hundred million dollars.

[36] The International Bank for Reconstruction and Development is more often referred to as the "World Bank." By December 27, 1945, all but seven of the countries represented at Bretton Woods had signed the Articles of Agreement. Subsequently three more have been admitted; the major country not accepting is the Soviet Union.

In 1949, the United States' gold stock mounted to an all-time peak of $24,771 million at the end of August. Since then the country has experienced a steady decline in its gold reserves, as Table 3.2 indicates. The amount of "free" gold available to meet the redemption demands upon dollar holdings of foreign governments and central banks had dwindled to an extremely low level by the end of January 1965. Additional gold reserves were "freed" by the Act of March 3, 1965, which eliminated the 25 percent gold-certificate reserve for liabilities other than Federal Reserve notes. At the time there was some debate as to whether or not Congress should also remove the gold reserve requirement for Federal Reserve notes; however, Congress seemed to fear that the public would become alarmed. Economic and political developments since 1965 indicated that within a short time people in the United States would return to a fiat money standard.

3.6. Fiat Money, March 18, 1968, to the Present

A continued drain of United States gold reserves, and the devaluation of the British pound sterling in late 1967 from the equivalent of $2.80 to $2.40, led President Lyndon B. Johnson in his 1968 State of the Union Address to "hint" strongly that the gold reserves behind the country's principal hand-to-hand money soon would have to be removed.

The conversion of dollars into gold by private speculators during the first few months of 1968 placed a large amount of pressure on the United States dollar in the international market. By March 14, the country's free gold reserves had dwindled to less than one-half billion dollars. On March 18 the President signed legislation releasing the 25 percent gold cover requirement for Federal Reserve notes, thus returning the country to a fiat money standard. The passage of the Act of

Table 3.2. Monetary Gold Reserves of the United States for Selected Years (in millions of dollars).

End of Year	Amount	End of Year	Amount
1949	24,563	1961	16,929
1950	22,879	1962	15,987
1956	21,942	1963	15,562
1957	22,769	1964	15,388
1958	20,563	1965	13,799
1959	19,482	1966	13,158
1960	17,954	1967	12,436

Source: *Federal Reserve Bulletins*, December 1959, and January 1968.

March 18, 1968, had few implications for the domestic economy. The United States maintained its support of the dollar in international markets, however, by continuing to allow conversion of dollars into gold by "official buyers" at the fixed price of $35 a fine ounce.

The Present System   Chapter Four
of Payment Media
in the
United States

Media of exchange in the United States have evolved into an extremely complex system of instruments, standards, habits, customs, and institutions. For the most part this treatise on payment media systems has dealt with "money" as a medium of exchange. Today, to a very large extent "credit" is used for purposes of exchange. In fact Hawtrey states that "Credit and money are both equally media of exchange." He states further that "Credit is often said to be a substitute for money." But, "It would be just as accurate to say that money is a substitute for credit. . . .[1] Accordingly this chapter is divided into analyses of money as a medium of exchange, and credit as a medium of exchange.

4.1. Money as a Medium of Exchange

It is generally accepted in economic and financial literature that the term "money" includes coin, currency, and demand deposits adjusted. As other instruments have become generally accepted as means of payment or as standards of value, however, there is an increasing tendency on the part of many modern economists to broaden the term "money" to include other instruments, particularly in empirical and theoretical analysis.[2] In a discussion of payment media systems that includes credit, it should make little difference whether "money" is used in a broad or narrow sense. Consequently, to avoid confusion the more generally accepted meaning of money is employed in this chapter.

4.1.1. Coins and Currency.

Coins and currency constitute the "hand-to-hand" money used by the public in small-denomination transactions.[3] The only types of currency presently issued are gold certificates

[1] R. G. Hawtrey, *Currency and Credit* (London: Longmans, Green, 1919), p. 16. A more detailed analysis of the relationship between money and credit is presented in the first section of Chapter 7.
[2] For example, Milton Friedman and Anna J. Schwartz, *A Monetary History of the United States, 1867–1960* (Princeton: Princeton University Press for the National Bureau of Economic Research, 1963) include in the term "money" all deposits of commercial banks including both demand and time deposits (see p. 4).
[3] For a complete list of the kinds of coin and currency used in the United States, see Appendix 3. It is important to note at this point that Congress has made all circulating United States coins and paper money legal

(issued only to Federal Reserve Banks), Federal Reserve notes, and United States notes (issued only to replace worn-out notes and the total amount outstanding may not be more than $357 million). All other types of outstanding currency are being retired, making the only important form of circulating currency Federal Reserve notes.

All coins presently issued are token money. The Coinage Act of 1965 provided for the issuance of token subsidiary coins: half-dollars, quarters, and dimes. Minor coins (nickels and pennies) and subsidiary coins are issued by the Treasury and paid to the Federal Reserve banks to accommodate public demand. The only coin issued today with any silver content is the half-dollar, and its silver content is so small as to be almost negligible.

The lack of "intrinsic" or commodity value in United States' subsidiary coins was a direct result of an increased demand for coins and industrial use of silver. In early 1959, the price of silver in the New York market rose above the Treasury's selling price. Consequently, the Treasury's stock of free silver dropped from 222 million ounces in April 1959 to 22 million ounces by the end of 1960. Additional upward pressure on prices in the silver market, combined with a depleted supply of free silver by 1965, led to the passage of the Coinage Act.

Additional demands for coins in recent years have been caused by an increased population and expanding business activity; for use in vending machines, telephones, and parking meters; for the payment of tolls and sales taxes; and by the hoarding of coins by coin collectors. These demands have increased the chore of the Treasury in supplying coins to meet public needs. The growth in the dollar amounts of coin and currency in circulation is shown in Table 4.1.

4.1.2. Demand Deposits Adjusted. "Demand deposits adjusted" means checking account balances in commercial banks other than interbank and United States Government deposits less cash items in the process of collection. Today, the check[4] as a written instrument is the primary means of transferring demand deposit balances and settling debts.

---

tender. Money that is legal tender is money which the law requires creditors to accept when tendered in payment of money obligations. "Checkbook money," which constitutes approximately 80 percent of the money supply, is generally accepted when proper identification is shown; however, this form of money does not possess the legal-tender quality.

[4] Technically a "check" is a bill of exchange. A bill of exchange is a written instrument drawn on one party ordering another party to pay to the order of a third party a sum certain in money. A check is a bill of exchange written by a payor, ordering a commercial bank in which he maintains a checking account to pay on demand a sum certain in money to the order of a payee. The legal conditions for negotiability are provided for in the Uniform Negotiable Instruments Act, which has been adopted by all the states, and more recently the Uniform Commercial Code, which has been adopted by all the states except one (Louisiana).

Table 4.1.   United States Coin and Currency in Circulation for Selected Years (in millions of dollars).

End of Year	Total in Circu-lation[a]	Coin and Small-Denomination Currency						
		Total	Coin	$1[b]	$2	$5	$10	$20
1939	7,598	5,553	590	559	36	1,019	1,772	1,576
1945	28,515	20,683	1,274	1,039	73	2,313	6,782	9,201
1955	31,158	22,021	1,927	1,312	75	2,151	6,617	9,940
1960	32,869	23,521	2,427	1,533	88	2,246	6,691	10,536
1961	33,918	24,388	2,582	1,588	92	2,313	6,878	10,935
1962	35,338	25,356	2,782	1,636	97	2,375	7,071	11,395
1963	37,692	26,807	3,030	1,722	103	2,469	7,373	12,109
1964	39,619	28,100	3,405	1,806	111	2,517	7,543	12,717
1965	42,056	29,842	4,027	1,908	127	2,618	7,794	13,369
1966	44,663	31,695	4,480	2,051	137	2,756	8,070	14,201

End of Year	Large-Denomination Currency						
	Total	$50	$100	$500	$1,000	$5,000	$10,000
1939	2,048	460	919	191	425	20	32
1945	7,834	2,327	4,220	454	801	7	24
1955	9,136	2,736	5,641	307	438	3	12
1960	9,348	2,815	5,954	249	316	3	10
1961	9,531	2,869	6,106	242	300	3	10
1962	9,983	2,990	6,448	240	293	3	10
1963	10,885	3,221	7,110	249	298	3	4
1964	11,519	3,381	7,590	248	293	2	4
1965	12,214	3,540	8,135	245	288	3	4
1966	12,969	3,700	8,735	241	286	3	4

[a] Outside Treasury and Federal Reserve Banks. Before 1955 details are slightly overstated because they include small amounts of paper currency held by the Treasury and the Federal Reserve Banks for which a denominational breakdown is not available.
[b] Paper currency only; $1 silver coins reported under coin.
Source: *Federal Reserve Bulletin*, January 1968.

Checks were first introduced in the United States in 1681 with a famous experiment called "The Fund at Boston in New England." "To meet the shortage of hard cash for trade, the businessmen of Boston mortgaged their land and wares to the fund, and in turn received a book credit against which they could draw checks." [5] There was some hope that the use of checks would spread among the public; however, checkbook money in the colonies was soon replaced by paper cur-

[5] *The Story of Checks* (New York: The Federal Reserve Bank of New York, 1962), 2nd ed., p. 7.

rency, which better suited the needs of the time. Only after the Revolutionary War, with the establishment of deposit banking, did checks come into widespread use.

Today checking-account balances in commercial banks constitute approximately 80 percent of the nation's total money supply and 90 percent of the dollar volume of transactions. The commercial banking system consummates money transfers through an elaborate clearing system for the settlement of deposit balances. Transfers of these balances are made when the payee presents to the bank a sight draft signed by the payor ordering his bank to pay on demand the stated sum of money. The institutional channels have been organized through which sixty to seventy million checks daily find their way physically from one to any other among over seventy million different accounts. A good portion of the work in a modern commercial bank is that entailed in handling these checks. It is estimated that each check on the average is transferred ten times. The elaborate organization for controlling the flow of these checks not only consists of individual banks' bookkeeping departments but also consists of the facilities of local clearinghouses, correspondent banks, and the Federal Reserve System.

When a bank cashes or receives for deposit checks drawn on a local bank, it can present them for payment through the local clearinghouse, but if a check is presented which is drawn on an out-of-town bank, it must look elsewhere for clearing facilities. Usually the bank will have three choices: (1) the check can be sent to the district Federal Reserve Bank, which will present the check to the drawee bank for payment; (2) it can send the check to a correspondent bank, which will present the check to the drawee bank; or (3) it can send the check directly to the drawee bank.

All member banks may employ the clearing facilities of the Federal Reserve System free of charge; state nonmember banks may also obtain free clearing services from the Federal Reserve by agreeing to remit checks at par and to keep with their district Federal Reserve bank balances sufficient to cover uncollectible items. The Federal Reserve banks pay one another for the results of their daily transactions by settling net balances. The final results of each day's net transfers among the Federal Reserve banks is made on the records of the Interdistrict Settlement Fund they maintain in Washington.

To illustrate the clearing process through the Federal Reserve System, let us suppose that Mrs. X, living in Albany, New York, buys a painting from an art dealer in Sacramento, California. (1) Having deposited funds in her account, (2) Mrs. X presents her check drawn on an Albany bank to the art dealer; (3) the dealer deposits the check in his

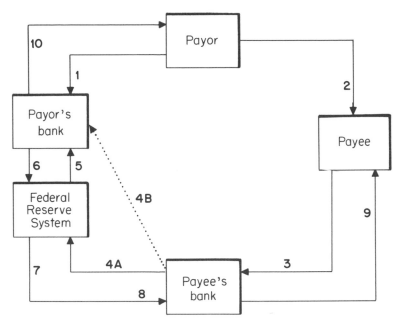

Figure 4.1. Diagram of the check-clearing process. (1) deposited funds; (2) check; (3) deposits check; (4A) check cleared through Federal Reserve System, or (4B) check sent to payor's bank; (5) check presented to bank; (6) authorization to deduct amount of check; (7) interdistrict settlement; (8) credit; (9) credit; (10) canceled check.

account at a Sacramento bank. (4) The Sacramento bank deposits the check for credit in its account at the Federal Reserve Bank of San Francisco; (5) The Federal Reserve Bank of San Francisco sends the check to the Federal Reserve Bank of New York for collection; (6) the Federal Reserve Bank of New York forwards the check to the Albany bank, which deducts the amount of the check from Mrs. X's account; (7) the Albany bank authorizes the Federal Reserve Bank of New York to deduct the amount of the check from its deposit account with the Reserve bank; (8) the Federal Reserve Bank of New York pays the Federal Reserve Bank of San Francisco by payment from its share in the Interdistrict Settlement Fund; (9) the Federal Reserve Bank of San Francisco credits the Sacramento bank's deposit account; (10) the Sacramento bank credits the art dealer's account.[6]

The check clearing process is reversed if the check is returned for insufficient funds or for some other reason by the payor's bank. Each year the process of check clearance becomes more cumbersome as the number of accounts and checks increase. Today the cost of handling

[6] *Ibid.*

checks for the banking system is estimated to be nearly $3.5 billion annually. The growth in checks processed annually and in the number of demand deposits are shown in Tables 4.2 and 4.3.

In the check-clearing process the Federal Reserve System can add to the primary reserves of the banking system; the net credit outstanding at any one time is known as Federal Reserve "float." Each Federal Reserve bank and branch has a set of time schedules which indicates whether immediate credit or deferred credit will be given for checks received. Usually checks which are drawn on banks located in close vicinity to a collecting Federal Reserve bank are given immediate credit; the maximum deferred time is two days. Presently, it is im-

Table 4.2. Number of Checks Processed Annually for Selected Years (numbers in billions).

Year	Number of Checks
1945	5.3
1950	7.0
1955	9.5
1960	12.7
1961	13.5
1962	14.3
1963	15.1
1964	16.0
1965	17.0
1966	18.0
1970	22.7

Source: American Bankers Association.

Table 4.3. Growth in Number of Demand-Deposit Accounts for Selected Years.

Year	Population	Number of Demand-Deposit Accounts
1936	136,362,000	22,109,000
1945	140,468,000	35,622,000
1955	165,931,000	52,212,000
1964	192,119,000	70,895,000
1970	210,000,000	85,000,000

Source: Federal Deposit Insurance Corporation; figures for 1970 are the writer's estimates.

possible for the Federal Reserve banks to collect all items within the time limits set for deferred credit items. Consequently, on the balance sheets of the Federal Reserve banks the item "cash items in process of collection" is greater than the item "deferred availability cash items." The difference between all of these items at any moment in time will represent free reserve credit to the banking system; this difference is the measure of Federal Reserve float.

Checks are written by a variety of different people and institutions for a variety of different purposes. One method by which checks may be analyzed is to consider the different classes of users of checks. It is useful in this regard to structure the payors and payees as belonging to one of three sectors in our society: individuals, businesses, and governments. Each of these sectors is involved in a check-writing relationship with the other sectors and with themselves. Therefore, there are nine relationship categories; examples in each category are found in the accompanying diagram. Although it is not possible to calculate the percentages of all checks written in each category, it has been determined that three of them account for the vast majority of all checks written. These three categories are businesses-to-individuals,

| | Payor | | |
Payee	Individuals	Businesses	Governments
Individuals	Services rendered Gifts Loans	Payrolls Dividends Pension payments	Welfare Social Security Payrolls Tax refunds
Businesses	Rent Mortgage payments Insurance Credit cards Supermarkets Loan payments	Payables	Loan payments
Governments	Tax payments	Tax payments Unemployment insurance Social Security insurance	Disbursements of federal programs

governments-to-individuals, and individuals-to-businesses.[7] Individuals occupy the central and most important position in the check-writing, check-receiving process. A study conducted by the Chase Manhattan Bank revealed the following conclusions concerning the ways in which individuals use checks:

1. Individuals are associated with the vast majority of checks in use either as payors or payees.

2. Individuals write approximately one-half of all checks, and the rate of growth of checks written by individuals is increasing faster than for other payors.

3. It is estimated that 57 percent of the checks written by individuals are sent through the mails.

4. The largest single category of checks which are mailed by individuals is for payments for charges incurred by credit cards.

5. Where joint accounts are in existence, women write approximately 62 percent of the checks drawn on those accounts.

6. Generally, when employees have been questioned as to whether they would desire to have their paychecks directly credited to a bank account, the answer has been "No." [8]

Governments, as well as individuals, write checks for a variety of purposes. The largest single check-writer is the federal government, which issues checks for Social Security payments, military payrolls, tax refunds, and miscellaneous purposes. The total number of federal government issued checks has increased substantially over the last several years, as indicated in Table 4.4.

Actually the use of demand deposits as money not only includes transfers made with checks and other credit instruments, but also checkless transfers of deposits. Banks will commonly debit deposit accounts for service charges, rent on safe-deposit boxes, and other amounts due banks. Many employers follow the practice of paying employees by arranging with their banks to credit the employees' accounts with their monthly salaries and to debit the employer's account with the gross amounts transferred. Arrangements are also made by many public utilities, insurance companies, and others with their customers to have their banks automatically credit the companies' accounts and debit the customers' accounts for recurring monthly payments. Arrangements such as these which are designed to increase customer convenience and reduce the volume of checks processed presently are being implemented

[7] Daniel Sitomer, "The Check — Its Role in the Checkless Society," in *Proceedings of the National Automation Conference* (New York: American Bankers Association, 1967), p. 260.
[8] *Ibid.*

Table 4.4. Federal Government Check Volume for Fiscal Years 1962–1966.

	1962	1963	1964	1965	1966
Social Security Payments	163,629,154	178,923,819	189,959,432	198,593,855	228,400,033
Military	95,657,059	94,918,825	94,188,926	96,266,037	98,965,049
Tax Refunds (Gas and Income)	40,470,741	40,704,667	42,362,861	39,841,453	45,311,179
Other	149,228,362	152,264,768	147,735,839	149,928,854	145,863,171
Total Checks Written	448,985,316	466,812,079	474,247,058	484,630,199	518,539,432

Source: United States Treasury Department.

by many banks across the country. Two of the more important techniques, bank credit cards and preauthorized payment systems, are discussed in considerable detail in Chapter 6.

At this point mention should be made of "wire transfers" of money balances. All of the Federal Reserve banks are linked together by a telegraph system that permits the Federal Reserve banks and all member banks to "wire" money free of charge if the amounts are in multiples of one hundred dollars. Wire transfers are simply coded messages instructing a Federal Reserve bank to transfer a certain sum of money on its records. Commercial wires are also used by the Federal Reserve to transfer sums of money for the accounts of banks, business firms, and individuals. No charge is incurred by the payor except for the cost of the necessary telegram. Additional transfers are made on the private wire facilities of some of the larger commercial banks.

It was recently announced that the Federal Reserve System will replace its nationwide teletypewriter network with a computerized system. The new system was planned to begin operations in November 1969. Initially the computer network will link the Federal Reserve Board of Governors, the Treasury Department, the twelve Federal Reserve banks, and the twenty-four branch banks. It was reported that the Board of Governors contemplates that the System's six thousand member commercial banks eventually will be tied in.

At present the teletype transfers average over 21,500 per day with an average daily volume in excess of twenty-six billion dollars. The new system will permit monetary data to be transferred at speeds up to forty times faster than the current network. The Board of Governors stated that "This will enable a vastly expanded volume of wire transfers of funds from one bank to another in supplement of — and perhaps, eventually, in substitute for, or replacement of — the huge and rapidly growing volume of transfers of money by check . . ." [9]

4.2. Credit as a Medium of Exchange

Basically "credit" means a promise to pay a sum of money sometime in the future in exchange for goods and services in the present. The credit system of the United States includes credit instruments, credit agencies, and laws and customs pertaining to the granting of credit and to the collecting of obligations. Since World War II, the United States' credit system has grown substantially in size and complexity in both the private and public sectors of the economy. Because of the character of recent developments in commercial banking and other financial institutions, the major focus of this study will be on consumer

[9] "Federal Reserve to Install Computerized Wire Links," *The Wall Street Journal,* February 28, 1968, p. 11.

credit. Consumer credit has been defined to include only credit issued to finance the purchase of goods and services for personal consumption or to refinance debts originally incurred for such purposes.

Consumer credit enables individuals in the marketplace to purchase commodities, benefit from their utility, and pay for them over a period of time in the future. The use of credit facilitates exchange in the present by postponing the payment in money; in many cases credit permits a transaction to occur which otherwise may not have been possible. Credit enables money to perform its function better.[10]

4.2.1. The Classification of Consumer Credit. The Federal Reserve Board classifies consumer credit by type of credit and type of holder. Installment credit is credit which is scheduled to be repaid in two or more installments and includes automobile loans, repair and modernization loans, personal loans, and other consumer-goods paper. Installment credit also includes revolving charge accounts and budget accounts which are paid in equal periodic installments. Approximately 80 percent of all consumer credit is installment credit. Noninstallment credit includes all other consumer credit; its major components are single-payment loans, charge accounts, and service credit.

Consumer credit is also classified under two major types of holders, financial institutions and retail outlets. Generally, credit originated by the former is referred to as "loan credit," and credit originated by the latter as "sale credit." The definitions used by the Federal Reserve Board in its compilation of consumer credit statistics are as follows:

"Automobile paper" and "other consumer goods paper" represent credit extended for the purpose of purchasing automobiles and other consumer goods and secured by the items purchased.

"Repair and modernization" include both FHA-insured and non-insured loans made to finance maintenance and improvement of owner-occupied dwelling units. These loans are used to finance the purchase and installation of equipment such as furnaces, hot water heaters, storm windows, and kitchen equipment, as well as major alterations and additions.

"Personal loans" include all instalment loans not covered in the previous categories made by financial institutions to individuals for consumer purposes. Most of these loans are for such purposes as consolidation of consumer debts, payment of medical, educational, or travel expenses, and payment of personal taxes and insurance premiums. Some personal loans are used for the purchase of consumer goods but they are not included under "automobile paper" or "other consumer goods paper" unless they are secured by the goods.

"Single-payment loans" are loans made to individuals for consumer

[10] Recall the fundamental purpose of money as described by Chandler, "to facilitate the exchange of goods and services — to lessen the time and effort required to carry on trade."

purposes and scheduled to be repaid in one payment. Most of the amount outstanding in this area is held by commercial banks. Small amounts are held by pawnbrokers, mutual savings banks, and savings and loan associations. While some credit of this type is used for the purchase of consumer goods, most is for meeting short-term needs such as the payment of personal taxes or life insurance premiums.

"Charge accounts" are the outstanding balances owed to retail dealers for purchases made by individuals for consumer purposes.

"Service credit" is the amount owed by individuals to professional practitioners and service establishments. The largest component of this type of credit is the amount owed by consumers to doctors, hospitals, and other medical practitioners. Amounts owed to public utilities, after deduction of deposits and prepayments, are another substantial component of service credit. The remainder represents amounts owed for a variety of personal services such as cleaning and dyeing, education, and recreation.[11]

4.2.2. The Recent Growth of Consumer Credit. Since the early 1920s total consumer installment credit has grown at a rate of about 9 percent annually. After World War II the rate of growth of consumer installment credit began to accelerate; in the first ten years after the war the growth rate approached 19 percent annually. In recent years individuals have increased their ability and willingness to commit future incomes to current consumption. The level of consumer credit depends mostly on the level of aggregate demand and personal, disposable income.

Both retail outlets and financial institutions have been motivated by profit considerations to increase the availability of consumer credit. Newer types of institutions such as credit unions and credit bureaus have come into existence to facilitate increased utilization of consumer credit. Retail establishments are able to increase sales volume by selling on credit, and many financial institutions such as commercial banks recently have begun to introduce new techniques in order to increase their share of the consumer credit market.

Other factors that have contributed to the growth of consumer credit include higher incomes, a general increase in the standard of living, an increase in leisure time, the shift of population to the suburbs, the introduction of new and improved consumer durable goods and services, a general increase of confidence in economic security, and a large growth in the number of people between twenty and thirty years of age who traditionally have been heavy users of consumer credit. Given the importance of material wealth to most American families and the high degree of competition and innovation in the area of consumer goods, the high rate of growth in consumer credit is almost certain to continue.

[11] James B. Ludtke, *The American Financial System* (Boston: Allyn and Bacon), 2nd ed., 1961, p. 376.

Table 4.5. Total Consumer Credit for Selected Years (in millions of dollars).

End of Year	Total	Installment					Noninstallment			
		Total	Automobile Paper	Other Consumer-Goods Paper	Repair and Modernization Loans[a]	Personal Loans	Total	Single-Payment Loans	Charge Accounts	Service Loans
1931	7,222	4,503	1,497	1,620	298	1,088	2,719	787	1,414	518
1941	9,172	6,085	2,458	1,929	376	1,322	3,087	845	1,645	597
1945	5,665	2,462	455	816	182	1,099	3,203	746	1,612	845
1960	56,028	42,832	17,688	11,525	3,139	10,480	13,196	4,507	5,329	3,360
1961	57,678	43,527	17,223	11,857	3,191	11,256	14,151	5,136	5,324	3,691
1962	63,164	48,034	19,540	12,605	3,246	12,643	15,130	5,456	5,684	3,990
1963	70,461	54,158	22,433	13,856	3,405	14,464	16,303	6,117	5,871	4,315
1964	78,442	60,548	25,195	15,593	3,532	16,228	17,894	6,954	6,300	4,640
1965	87,884	68,565	28,843	17,693	3,675	18,354	19,319	7,682	6,746	4,891
1966	94,786	74,656	30,961	19,834	3,751	20,110	20,130	7,844	7,144	5,142

[a] Holdings of financial institutions; holdings of retail outlets are included in "other consumer-goods paper."
Source: *Federal Reserve Bulletin*, January 1968.

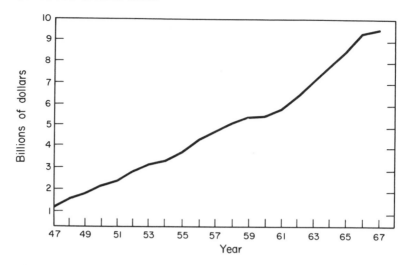

Figure 4.2. Total consumer credit (1947–1967).

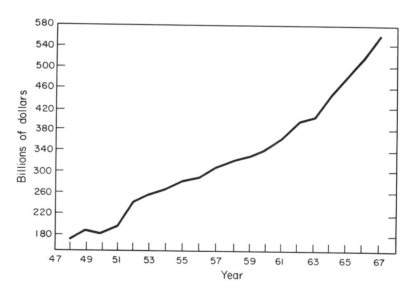

Figure 4.3. Disposable income (1947–1967).

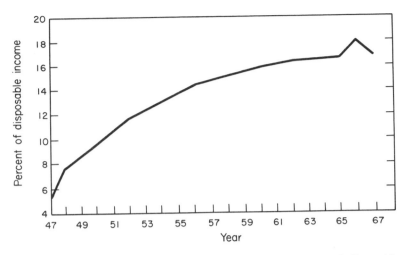

Figure 4.4. Total consumer credit outstanding as a percent of disposable income (1947–1967).

The recent growth of installment and noninstallment consumer credit by major types of credit is shown in Table 4.5. Figures 4.2, 4.3, and 4.4, respectively, indicate by means of graphs the growth of total consumer credit, disposable income, and the percent of consumer credit to disposable income from 1947 to 1967.

**The Evolution
and Current Status
of the Nonbank
Credit Card**

Chapter Five

In recent years, the credit card has become the major device for the substitution of credit for cash and checks at the retail level.[1] Usually the customer presents his card to the merchant, who records the type of purchase, the dollar amount, and the cardholder's assigned credit number. Once a month the consumer receives a statement with copies of his sales chits, and often he has the option of remitting in full or paying a portion thereof, which automatically extends his liability to a deferred-payment basis with an interest charge computed on the outstanding balance. The credit card saves the consumer the nuisance of cash or check disbursements with each purchase and provides him with an accurate record of purchases and expenses for tax and other purposes. Not only have private credit-card organizations emerged, which now number their memberships in the hundreds of thousands, but most large retailers and petroleum companies have developed their own credit-card departments.

For the purpose of this chapter, which is to present an analysis of the evolution and current status of the credit card, it will be useful to divide credit cards into three major groups: (1) cards issued for travel and entertainment, (2) cards issued by petroleum companies, and (3) cards issued by retailers (other than for travel and entertainment, or issued by petroleum companies).

5.1. Credit Cards Issued for Travel and Entertainment

The industrial boom after Warld War II created an untold number of new markets and gave rise to several innovations designed to fulfill many newly developed wants. The travel and entertainment credit card met the needs of corporate executives who wanted purchasing power convenience and accurate records of company and personal charges.

Today, a major travel and entertainment credit card enables the businessman to "charge" virtually all but pocket-change expenses encountered on a typical business trip. The sponsoring organization issues

[1] This paragraph is adapted with minor changes from D. W. Richardson, "Technological Innovation in the Future of Commercial Banking," *Business Studies,* Fall 1967, p. 75.

a card to people of high credit standing (usually there are minimum income and other requirements) and encourages motels, hotels, clubs, restaurants, nearly all types of firms engaged in transportation, and many others to honor its credit card. Sales are generally made at a discount, and the merchants' accounts receivable are transferred to the card sponsor, who in turn assumes responsibility for collections and bad-debt losses. The merchant participates in the plan because he feels sales revenue will increase, and he is willing to pay (in the form of a discount) for the privilege of accepting the credit card and transferring his receivables to the credit-card company.

The credit-card company generally earns a return from two major sources. The primary source is the merchant discount, which in many cases is as high as 10 percent and more. The second source is from initial and annual fees paid by the credit cardholders for the privilege of using the card. This fee is generally a flat sum ranging from five to twenty-five dollars annually.

Many businesses have entered the travel and entertainment credit-card industry. From the standpoint of size, however, ". . . there are only three firms which have an important stake in this expanding field. Diners' Club, Incorporated, American Express Company, and Hilton Credit Corporation [Carte Blanche] have survived the shake-out which, over the past several years saw a number of firms fall by the wayside as competitive pressures mounted." [2]

5.1.1. Diners' Club. Diners' Club was the pioneer in the travel and entertainment credit-card field; the company's first card was issued in 1950.[3] As with most firms in a new industry, inexperience generates many costly errors. The initial costs of the Diners' Club operation were high, and a large charge volume was the only way of reaching and surpassing the break-even point. Volume was encouraged through large advertising and promotional outlays and by issuing credit cards to individuals with only marginal credit ratings. Consequently, the first several years of operation were not successful in terms of profitability.

Fortunately for Diners' Club there was no competition, and bad credit risks and promotional costs eventually waned. Shortly after Diners' Club began earning a profit, new firms began to enter the market. In 1958, American Express Company and Hilton Credit Corporation entered the credit-card business.

In 1960 Diners' Club had 1.1 million members and a charge volume of over $165 million annually. However, in less than two years American Express Company had built its credit-card charge volume to

[2] "Credit Cards Are Here to Stay," *Financial World,* March 27, 1963, p. 6.
[3] "Credit Cards Companies Come Into the Chips," *Business Week,* September 4, 1965, p. 54.

over $100 million and had signed up 750,000 members. Hilton Credit Corporation's Carte Blanche credit card reported in 1960 that its 400,000 members were running up charges at the rate of $100 million annually.[4] By early 1961, Diners' Club showed signs of losing its leading position. In 1962, the firm had about 60,000 member establishments and 1.25 million member cardholders throughout the world. Approximately one million card holders were in the United States and Canada, and total yearly billings were approximately $200 million.

New ventures undertaken in the early 1960s led Diners' Club into commercial financing and factoring. However, instead of providing growth, by 1964 losses on those ventures exceeded a half million dollars after taxes. Total earnings by Diners' Club that year were $2.2 million. In November 1964, Ralph E. Schneider, the company's president, died and cofounder Alfred Bloomingdale succeeded him in the position as chief executive. An analysis of the firm's problems prompted Mr. Bloomingdale to comment, "We found out we were experts in lending 1,000 guys $10, but not one guy $10,000." [5]

By 1965, charge volume had gained substantially, primarily due to a wider range of customer services. Computer billings were started in September 1965, which temporarily increased the company's fixed and operating expenses. Direct costs associated with converting to computers were $486,000 over a three-year period; estimated indirect costs, however, were near $1.5 million.[6] The newer customer services included the company's "custom credit-card" operations. Under service contracts, Diners' Club began to manage charge accounts and revolving credit plans identified with other organizations.[7]

Today, Diners' Club operates charge accounts and revolving credit plans with other organizations under service contracts. Such services are operated for Budget-Rent-A-Car Systems, Jack Tar Hotel-Motel, The Gaslight Clubs, and others. The Diners' Club cardholder can also charge air travel expenses with more than thirty airlines and buy merchandise from a select number of mail-order firms. An increased charge volume and more prudent credit extension policies have improved the market and profit position of Diners' Club. Delinquent-account losses dropped from 2 percent in 1961 to 0.1 percent in 1965.[8]

In the later part of 1965, it was announced that the Chase Manhattan Bank of New York (which once operated its own credit-card business and sold to Uni-Serv in 1962) agreed to pay roughly $56.5 million for

---

[4] "Tougher Going for Credit Cards," *Business Week*, September 4, 1965, p. 54.
[5] "Lagging Leader," *Forbes*, October 15, 1965, p. 44.
[6] *Ibid.*
[7] "Credit Card Shakeout," *Financial World*, January 13, 1965, p. 22.
[8] "Lagging Leader," *Forbes*, p. 45.

the Diners' Club operation.[9] However, because of a skeptical attitude from the Justice Department and for other reasons the purchase of Diner's Club by the Chase did not materialize.

5.1.2. American Express Company. American Express Company entered the credit-card industry in 1958, and although it built up over $100 million of sales volume in less than two years, the company was still losing money in 1960.[10] Startup costs were mainly responsible for the company's losses for several years after beginning operation. In the years 1961–1963, credit-card charge volume had increased at a rate of 26 percent annually, and by 1964, charge volume had jumped 40 percent to an estimated $340 million, up from $240 million in 1963.[11]

In mid-1963, American Express Company began a joint study with American Airlines of the charge market for air travel expenses, and the outgrowth of their efforts was the company's new "Sign & Fly" service. Under their plan, an American Express cardholder can charge air fares at an airline ticket office or at any American Express travel agent simply by presenting his card and signing his name. Cardholder members have the option of being billed on either a current monthly basis or through extended payments ranging up to twelve months. In less than a year American Express Company had signed up 56 airlines including ten foreign lines.

By 1965, American Express Company enjoyed a commanding lead in the travel and entertainment credit-card field. On December 24, 1965, the firm acquired Uni-Serv Corporation, a retail credit-card system in New York City. At the time Uni-Serv had approximately 650,000 cardholders, and it became a wholly owned subsidiary of American Express Company. In early 1962, Uni-Serv, then just a corporate shell, had acquired the Chase Manhattan Bank's Charge Plan in New York.[12] Uni-Serv was started by Joseph P. Williams, a former vice-president of the Bank of America. With backing from a financial syndicate put together by Shearson, Hammill Company, Uni-Serv paid only slightly over $8.8 million for almost an exact amount of the Chase's receivables. With the purchase of Uni-Serv, American Express Company obtained substantial interests in both the travel and entertainment and the retail credit-card fields.

5.1.3. Carte Blanche Corporation. The Hilton Credit Corporation acquired the Carte Blanche credit card from Hilton Hotels in the latter part of 1958. During its first full year of operations Carte Blanche reported a loss of $2.4 million, of which at least $800,000 was in bad-debt

[9] "Credit Card Kaleidoscope," *Financial World*, December 15, 1965, p. 14.
[10] "Tougher Going for Credit Cards," *Business Week*, p. 49.
[11] "Credit Card Shakeout," *Financial World*, p. 11.
[12] See "New Shuffle in Credit Cards," *Business Week*, November 3, 1962, p. 65.

expenses. Even though credit sales volume was up to $110 million annually by 1960, delinquencies were the company's major problem. Hilton Credit Corporation's credit director, Joseph Tilem, admitted, ". . . that when the company conceived the idea of the Carte Blanche, it made an unfortunate oversight — it forgot the credit angle. New accounts weren't processed carefully, and the company lacked adequate credit-checking in the stores where the credit was being extended." [13]

By mid-1960, Carte Blanche reported a profit of $116,000. However, Tilem attributed the company's profit to improvements in operating costs rather than to a reduction in delinquencies. Tilem said that during this period there was an increasing tendency for credit cardholders to "kite" credit through their credit cards. He stated that "Studies have shown . . . that 75% of credit-cardholders have more than one card." He claimed that many of the delinquents were using Diners' Club one month, Carte Blanche the next, and "Amex" the following month. "By stalling first one company and then another, the card holder can postpone a long time his day of reckoning, when he has to pay up or be sued." [14]

Hilton Credit Corporation failed to achieve a profitable year until 1963, and in 1964 the company earned $2.3 million. Earnings per share of common stock increased substantially in 1965; however, Hilton was still able to deduct tax loss carryforwards from preceding years' deficit operations so as to avoid paying taxes on reported profits in these later years.[15] By 1965, it was estimated that Carte Blanche had between 350,000 and 400,000 member cardholders. In addition Hilton Credit Corporation serviced about the same number of Hilton Hotel credit cards for the parent Hilton Hotel Corporation, making their total number of outstanding credit cards close to one million.

It was announced in the later part of 1965 that the First National City Bank of New York would pay some $12 million for the voting stock of a new corporation to operate Carte Blanche.[16] During the same year Carte Blanche extended its service when Phillips 66 Service Stations agreed to honor its card and when American Airlines also agreed to accept Carte Blanche. Citibank controlled Carte Blanche from December 31, 1965, until April 8, 1968, when it was sold to the Avco Corporation, a diversified company with considerable interests in consumer financing.

5.2. Credit Cards Issued by Petroleum Companies

The petroleum industry was the major pioneer in the credit-card

---

[13] "Tougher Going for Credit Cards," *Business Week,* p. 49.
[14] *Ibid.*
[15] "Credit Card Shakeout," *Financial World,* p. 23.
[16] "Credit Card Kaleidoscope," *Financial World,* p. 14.

field. In the early 1930's paper cards, usually issued every three to six months, could be used to purchase gasoline and a few minor automotive services. By 1940, credit-card purchases from many companies were extended to include tires, batteries, and other assorted accessories. In the late 1950s and early 1960s many oil-company credit cards were being used to purchase goods and services having no apparent relationship to the petroleum industry. Today, "oil" credit cards can be used to charge automobile repairs, restaurant and motel charges, life and accident insurance, sporting goods, boats and outboard motors, air conditioners and a host of other products and services.[17]

The era of rapid growth in petroleum-company credit cards was the decade of the 1950's. In the five-year period 1952 to 1957, there was a 50 percent increase in the total number of petroleum-company credit-card holders;[18] in the latter 1950s the number of many companies' cardholders continued to grow at a rate greater than 20 percent annually. During this period when 25 to 30 percent of the retail oil industry's business was transacted through the use of credit cards, the plastic credit card was introduced.[19]

The new plastic card could be inserted in an imprinter that reproduced the cardholder's name and account number on a sales ticket. Although costs initially were increased for most companies that bought or rented imprinters, consumer appeal led to increased sales. With the plastic card the time required to record a sale was decreased, and cards began to be issued on a nonexpiring basis.

During this same period, advancements made in electronic data-processing equipment led to internal changes and cost savings in many oil companies. Most major companies had converted to centralized credit accounting systems by the early 1960s. Socony Mobil, for example, reduced the number of its retail accounting offices from seventeen to four when it installed an automated credit system.

The development of the optical scanner in the early 1960s enabled firms to reduce the number of required keypunch operators and to cut costs. The optical scanner can "read" account numbers from credit-card invoices and automatically punch a computer card. The scanner can read and punch over 10,000 cards per hour compared with 850 cards per hour for the average keypunch operater.[20] In 1960, the Humble

[17] "Expanded Use of Oil Credit Cards," *National Petroleum News,* December 1964, p. 99.
[18] "New Ideas Are Coming Fast," *National Petroleum News,* December 1957, p. 94.
[19] See "Boosting Credit Card Sales," *National Petroleum News*, March 1957, p. 94.
[20] See "New Revolution in Credit-Card Processing," *National Petroleum News,* November 1965.

Oil and Refining Company and Gulf Oil Corporation began testing a barcode system developed by the Addressograph-Multigraph Company that would eliminate nearly all manual work. The new system, substantially implemented in the industry by 1965, replaced the pressure-type imprinters, which recorded only the cardholder's name and account number. The newer imprinters permitted the service station attendant to set the amount of the sale by machine. The scanner then reads the invoices and punches out *all* the necessary data. In 1965, Texaco reportedly acquired 50,000 of the newer station imprinters, and Humble Oil had approximately 30,000 stations equipped with these devices.[21]

Today, most major oil companies have completely automatic credit and accounting systems. A typical example of how electronic data-processing equipment can automate a firm's credit-card activities is presented now in a brief description of the system implemented by the Marathon Oil Company.

5.2.1. Marathon Oil Company's Automated Credit-Card System. By 1966, Marathon Oil's credit-card activities had resulted in an unmanageable mass of paper work. At the same time retail gasoline industry competition necessitated the company's mailing out over 16,000 new credit cards per month. The corporation's management undertook a complete revision of the firm's accounting and data-processing departments, and implemented a new system which included an International Business Machines 1401 computer, optical scanners, sorters, collators, microfilming recorders, and accounting and proving machines.

Invoices are now prepared at the service stations by Addressograph-Multigraph code imprinters. The imprinter records the cardholder's name and account number, and the amount of the sale is registered in a code of vertical bars. Service station operators mail the invoices into the company's headquarters in Findlay, Ohio, every three or four days. "The invoices are immediately put through a series of accounting steps aimed at mailing payment to the dealer the next day and statements to motorists in keeping with an eight-cycle, four-day billing schedule." [22] The invoices are dated and numbered by a Bitney-Bowes endorsing machine, microfilmed by a Recordak camera, and then scanned by the Addressograph-Multigraph code reader.

[21] "What Scanners Are Doing for Humble," *National Petroleum News,* November 1965, p. 129.
[22] "Machines Move Mountains For Paper-Ridden Marathon," *National Petroleum News,* September 1966, p. 132.

After being scanned, the invoices are balanced by an International Business Machines sorter, sorted to eliminate special accounts (company employees, etc.), and again sorted by customer number. A "dummy" card is substituted for any nonpayable items, and operators manually keypunch the small percentage of invoices rejected by the scanner. Finally, a small crew of workers must balance the dealer transmission cards that are out of balance with the totaled invoices.

The investment in computer and data-processing equipment proved successful for Marathon as it did for most oil companies. Credit-card invoices can be processed quickly and easily. Dealers receive payment early; motorists are billed promptly; payment is received quickly; and accounts receivable are held to a minimum. In less than one year after automating its credit system, Marathon Oil increased the number of its outstanding credit cards from 420,664 to 610,362 cards.

5.2.2. The Increasing Credit-Card Problems of the Petroleum Industry. Despite the considerable growth of aggregate gasolines sales volume and the credit-processing cost reductions experienced by most firms, the industry's credit-card activities have resulted in several major problems for the petroleum companies. Because of the enormity of the credit-card activities of the petroleum industry and because of the industry's approximate three and one-half decades of experience in this rapidly growing area, it should prove useful to examine some of these problem areas in some detail.

One of the major credit-card problems of the petroleum industry has been and continues to be the cost of offering and processing consumer credit. Initially it is costly to start an account. In 1959, the *Oil and Gas Journal* reported, "To place a credit-card in force costs from $1.89 to $5 before a nickel's worth of product is sold." [23] Once an account is opened the costs continue to increase. In 1964, for example, Coast Oil Company of San José, California, reported that its credit-card business cost about 2.3 cents per gallon of gasoline, and in 1962, the costs had been approximately 4 cents per gallon. According to Coast Oil the lower figure amounted to about 7 percent of its total dollar credit-card volume, the higher figure about 12 percent.[24] One major oil company marketer summed up what he felt to be the "dilemma of credit-cards" when he said, "Credit cards cost a fortune, but you have to have them. They do build gallonage, although admittedly at a cost.

[23] "Where Credit-Card Buying Is Headed," *The Oil and Gas Journal,* September 9, 1959, p. 63.
[24] "How a Private-Brand Jobber Controls Credit-Card Costs," *National Petroleum News,* April 1964, p. 108.

In the long run, if you tried to build the same gallonage by gimmicking or cutting price, market deterioration would lose you what you'd gained." 25

The preceding cost figures appear even more staggering when one is presented with the fact that better than one-half of the over 100 million petroleum company credit cards outstanding are classified as "inactive." The average motorist has from three to seven cards at his command. "If a company has 1,700,000 cards in force, chances are not over 700,000 are used regularly. If $2 is an average cost of setting up the account, the company has invested $2,000,000 on which there is no return." While the demand for gasoline is increasing at a rate in the neighborhood of 3 to 5 percent annually, the credit business is increasing at a yearly rate of 15 to 18 percent.26 In 1964, it was reported that the number of credit cards outstanding was expected to continue to grow at a rate of approximately 15 percent per year. One expert said that the number of valid credit cards should double within ten years; for each of the major oil companies, ". . . this will mean 7-million or 8-million card-holders." 27

Despite the fact that computers and electronic data processing equipment have managed to cut the costs of processing credit, by the mid-1960s processing costs appeared to reach their minimum. "Ten years ago, a national major's processing costs accounted to 4.8% of total credit-card purchases. In 1962 costs were down to 2.6% last year [1963], 2.5%. 'We've gone about as far as we can go,' said one company [official] in 1964." 28 *National Petroleum News* reported that because of the efficiency of most modern electronic data processing systems, increased numbers of customers did not contribute significantly to a reduction in per unit costs. In 1964, one oil company spokesman estimated that, ". . . a 30% increase in the number of card-holders would cut the company's per unit costs only 0.1%." 29

Today, one of the major problems facing the petroleum industry is the increasing number of inactive credit cards outstanding. In mid-1967, the Gulf Oil Corporation discovered that approximately 56 percent of its eleven million credit-card holders failed to use their cards even once in a given month. Gulf Oil is not alone; recently nearly all oil companies have been experiencing similar problems. The industry's high proportion of inactive credit cards has been attributed to three

25 *Ibid.*
26 "Where Credit-Card Buying Is Headed," *The Oil and Gas Journal,* p. 63.
27 "Credit-Card Bonanza — and the Cost of Exploiting It," *National Petroleum News,* October 1964, p. 101.
28 *Ibid.*
29 *Ibid.*

major factors: (1) flooding of the public with unsolicited credit cards, many of which will never be used; (2) inconvenience of station location to the card-holder; and (3) the growing inclination of motorists to own six or eight or a dozen different oil-company credit cards.[30]

Companies define "inactive" credit card-holders differently, but there are two basic yardsticks: no purchase for a month; and no purchase for twelve months. Those companies which use the twelve-month system include Marathon Oil, 59 percent inactive accounts; Citgo, 51 percent, and Continental Oil, 49 percent. The percentages naturally tend to be higher for those companies using a monthly or similar close-check system; those oil companies include Sunray DX, 66 percent inactive; Phillips Petroleum Company, 60 percent; Atlantic division of Atlantic Richfield, 60 percent; Gulf Oil Corporation, 56 percent; and the American Oil Company, 50 percent.

The problem of inactive credit cards began to receive widespread attention from the petroleum industry in the early 1960s. In 1964, it was reported that oil-company marketing men were making an all-out attack on the problems surrounding credit-card operations by offering nonoil merchandise at discounts to credit cardholders. Although companies hoped to increase business at their stations and make a profit on selling the merchandise, their main aim was to make active customers of inactive cardholders. The result: "Merchandise running the gamut from cameras to kitchen utensils, from golf balls to hair-dryers, is being offered at discounts to major-company credit-card holders. Some companies are even offering insurance and baseball tickets." [31]

What Ten Petroleum Companies Have Tried in Order to Help Solve the Problem of Inactive Credit Cards Mid-1960s[32]

Pure Oil has had a series of multiple-merchandise mailings to credit-card customers. Last spring its multiple mailing offered five products to active and inactive accounts, with inactives required to validate forms.

Pure billed this promotion as a "Spring Shopping Spectacular." The products included a Sportline sleeping bag ($8.99), Dairybar mixer for milk and ice cream drinks ($9.99), Melamine dinnerware set ($8.89), Dominion coffee-maker ($9.59), and a portable tape recorder ($27.27). All but the tape recorder had to be bought on a one-payment plan; the recorder was available for three $9.37 payments. Billing was on the regular monthly statement.

[30] See "Oil's Credit Puzzle: How to Get Millions to Use Their Cards," *National Petroleum News*, June 1967, p. 92.
[31] "Credit-Card Merchandising: Can It Stop the Cost Spiral?" *National Petroleum News*, October 1964, p. 100.
[32] "What 10 Companies Are Doing, What They Sell, How, To Whom," *National Petroleum News*, October 1964, pp. 105–106.

Only holders of inactive cards were required to have a Pure dealer validate the order form.

Mobil Oil has tested the impact of merchandise offers to credit-card customers through separate mailings on three products. Mobil made regional offers on a coffee pot ($9.98), ladies' electric shaver ($8.88), and hair dryer ($19.98). The coffee-pot promotion, which proved the most successful of the three, was repeated in other markets.

All three offers were on a single-payment plan with charges built into the cardholder's monthly statement. All orders had to be validated at a station, but no purchase was required. The offers were made to all accounts.

Kerr-McGee tested a direct-mail merchandise promotion a year ago when it sent its Deep Rock credit-card holders "a special Christmas offer" of nine different items in prices ranging from $3.75 to $19.90.

To make a purchase a card-holder took an order blank to a Deep Rock dealer and had it validated. After validation, the customer sent a check or money order along with the filled-out order form to International Manor Ltd., a Los Angeles company specializing in credit-card merchandise services. The mailing went to all accounts.

Included in Kermac's multiple-product offer were a Lady Sunbeam electric shaver ($6.90), Dormeyer hand mixer ($8.75), Sunbeam fry pan ($16.50), Westinghouse hair dryer ($19.90), Ronson shoeshine kit ($14.90), Ronson can opener/knife sharpener ($17.50), Raleigh transistor radio ($7.95), Sunbeam cordless toothbrush set ($11.75), and a doll set ($3.75).

Signal Oil & Gas offered its active credit-card customers a battery-operated phonograph, manufactured by North American Phillips Co., in a pre-Christmas mailing last year. The price, including $25 worth of records, was $39.95, comparable to a $64.95 value, the company says.

To get the phonograph, a card-holder simply had to fill out an order form and mail it in. Billing was on the card-holder's regular monthly statement. No station validation was required. Customers could buy up to two phonographs, a limit designed to minimize credit risks.

Signal O&G's phonograph offer was also available for cash purchase at Hancock, Regal, and Norwalk stations.

Continental Oil offered its credit-card customers a selection of 12 plants, all guaranteed to grow, in a mailing held in the summer and autumn of 1962. For from 50¢ to $1 per plant, cardholders could buy dwarf banana trees, miniature roses, and pine trees, among others. Orders were mailed directly to the supplier, which notified Conoco for billing purposes. No validation was required, with inactives required to validate forms.

Sunray DX has staged one direct-mail merchandise promotion, a multiple-product mailing between Sept. 1 and Dec. 31, 1963, offering credit-card holders a variety of Mirro aluminum cook ware. To buy the merchandise, a card-holder had to place the order on a special form and mail it in. Billing was on the card-holder's regular monthly department which ordered the merchandise from the manufacturer. Mirro sent the items directly to the customer. The card-holder was billed on his regular monthly statement.

Four items were sold: a 35-cup percolator ($11.50), 11-in. electric skillet ($10.75), 14-piece copperware set ($13.95), and an electric corn popper ($7.40).

Union Oil of California ran a special Christmas mailing last year, offering credit-card accounts a variety of "Mission Pak Sampler," priced at $5.96 and containing "generous servings" of fruit cake, date-and-nut cake, glaceed fruits, dates, and preserves. No validation was required.

Shell Oil has recently conducted a series of test mailings to inactive and active card-holders. "Our testing has been done on a limited basis. Results are still being studied to determine whether we should go ahead," a Shell spokesman says.

Shell has had at least five separate mailings, offering a circular saw ($19.95) on a three-payment plan, Swiss watch (three payments), Kodak camera and film, fishing tackle, and model trains. Customers had to validate orders.

Richfield Oil (California) has made two merchandise offers to credit-card holders. The first, staged last year, was a multiple mailing selling a carving set and salad set, among other merchandise. More recently, Richfield has offered its 1-million card holders a Kodak "Hawkeye Instamatic" camera, valued at $12.95, for $7. The promotion, which started in June, will last until January 31, 1965.

Richfield's offer was made to active accounts and inactive accounts with no credit problems, but under separate mailings. Validation was required.

Richfield has also developed a follow-up system designed to further stimulate credit-card activity. With each camera shipment, a special order form and brochure are enclosed, offering the customer additional equipment, including a flash attachment ($2.50) and camera case ($2.50).

American Petrofina is another company that mailed credit-card customers a pre-Christmas offer, part of promotion available to all Fina customers. In conjunction with Purolator Products, which arranged and sponsored the promotion, and Instant Bonus, which processed and filled orders, Fina card-holders were offered such products as a rod and reel, hair dryer, electric hedge trimmer, and floor polisher, ranging in price from $9.95 to $19.95. If a customer wanted to place an order, he had to validate the order blank at a Fina station, then mail it with a check or money order to Instant Bonus.

By using merchandising programs, oil marketers felt that once an inactive cardholder uses his card to buy merchandise, he is more likely to start charging gasoline, oil, and other purchases at the company's service stations. Oil companies had varying degrees of success with their merchandising programs; none, however, was extremely rewarding. One merchandising man calculated the minimum response levels in order to break even on its discount merchandise to be 5 percent from active cardholders and 2 percent from inactive cardholders.

National Petroleum News in October 1964 reported, "One major's promotion enticed only 1.6% of its cardholders into replying. Another company's offer had a response ratio of 1.32 per thousand cardholders in one region, far below expectations." Some companies reported more favorable results. One major oil company had mixed responses; ". . . 3.5% on one offer, less than 2% on three others." [33] Shell Oil reportedly had a 6 percent overall response on one mailing. Richfield (California) estimated total orders on a seven-dollar camera to be in the neighborhood of a 11 percent response from total company credit cards outstanding.

By 1967, the costs of setting up an account had decreased to an estimated $1.00 to $1.25. There are also costs involved in running a credit check on a potential customer; a Mobil Oil Company official claims the credit check costs more than setting up an account.[34] During the course of a single year a major petroleum company is likely to issue over one million new cards. Company officials feel that their cardholders are so important, however, that most firms carry inactive credit cards for years. The Gulf Oil Company used to mail out elaborate messages to its inactive cardholders every six months; now the company waits two years before sending out a subtle inquiry. Even if a company suddenly wanted to attack its inactive list it would be extremely difficult, for nonexpiring cards are now in vogue.

Company managements tend to think that the best solution to the inactive credit-card problem is to attempt to stimulate inactives to make purchases. Somehow they think there still exists some "link" between the oil company and its inactive credit cardholders. Just suppose that the Gulf Oil Company could magically induce its six million-plus inactive cardholders to buy a single tank of gasoline apiece; it would create approximately twenty million dollars in sales revenues. Such a dream appears too enticing for most oil company officials to abandon. Experience makes it seem doubtful, however, that merchandising schemes could promote much of an increase in credit-card usage. By analyzing the economics of a merchandising program one company official explained that "An oil company can't get more than $1 from a $10 sale. . . . And a 5% return on 1-million cards . . . a high return considering results so far would net $50,000. At 5¢ per mailing, that's exactly what postage would cost." [35]

Another serious credit-card problem facing the oil industry is the increasing number of lost and stolen credit cards. An American Oil

[33] "Credit-Card Merchandising: Can It Stop the Cost Spiral?" *National Petroleum News*, p. 103.
[34] "Oil's Credit Puzzle: How to Get Millions to Use Their Cards," *National Petroleum News*, p. 93.
[35] "Credit-Card Merchandising: Can It Stop the Cost Spiral?" *National Petroleum News*, p. 103.

Company official pointed out in 1965 that even though the percentage of lost credit cards that were misused was small, "every time we pick up a bad one we save about $500." The misuse of cards can prove very costly. American Oil experienced a case where a ring of credit-card thieves ran up a bill of ten thousand dollars. "The record for a single individual bad credit-card with an oil company is reportedly $24,000." [36] In 1965, a new system established in the New York metropolitan area called Telecheck was designed to minimize losses from misused oil credit cards. On sales of over twenty-five dollars the participating dealer telephones a local Telecheck number. Upon receiving the suspicious credit-card number, the operator types the number into an International Business Machines 1440 computer, which in turn checks the number against all known bad credit cards. If the number turns up bad, the dealer attempts to make the card-holder's automobile immobile. The dealer then consummates the sale and reports the transaction to local authorities for prosecution. For the service Telecheck initially bills the oil company $1.50 per dealer, plus a charge of $1.50 per dealer per month.

In addition to credit-card counterfeiting certain "gimmicks" are being used which increase the cost of credit cards to the petroleum industry. Recently, it was reported that certain independent car washes in the Los Angeles area were "swapping" oil company credit. *National Petroleum News* reported:

Some car-wash operators advertise on curb signs that they will accept certain major credit-cards, and then swap invoices with car washes of other brands or peddle invoices at a discount to service stations of the brand uses. . . . For example, one car wash with Shell pumps advertises, "All major credit cards accepted except Standard" of California. Consider the case of a driver with a Union Oil credit card who comes in for a wash and fills up on Shell gasoline.

The car-wash clerk tickets the total purchase, gasoline plus wash, on a Union Oil credit invoice, but leaves off the name of the establishment. Later the car-wash operator takes all Union Oil invoices and swaps or sells them at Union car washes or stations or both.

The Union car wash or service station runs the invoice through its own imprinter and submits it along with all its other invoices for full credit. One report says discounts are up to 30% of face value. A 3% rate is said to be standard.

What bothers the oil companies, of course, is that their credit cards can be used to buy some other company's products or services. The company is being bilked of the cost of the credit.[37]

[36] "Is That Credit Card Any Good?" *National Petroleum News*, November, 1965, p. 112.

[37] "Credit-Swapping at Car Washes Bothers Majors in Los Angeles," *National Petroleum News*, July 1966, p. 39.

In an attempt to solve some of the oil industry's credit-card troubles several movements have been organized to promote a single, universal credit card. One attempt by Frontier Refining Company of Denver was made as early as 1949.[38] Under the Frontier plan authorized dealers were allowed to accept sales made on "foreign" credit cards (cards of other oil companies) with a 6 percent charge levied on the dealer. Because of insufficient research, however, dealers had no idea of how much extra business was needed to justify a universal acceptance plan.

National Credit Card, Incorporated, initiated a universal petroleum credit card in 1951. Oil companies would agree to accept the card with a 6 percent service charge and a twenty-dollar dealer-paid membership fee. At that time the major companies did not want to give up their investment in their own credit-card operations, and interest was generated seriously by only the private-brand oil jobbers and the smaller companies with no existing credit-card arrangements.

Reportedly three major obstacles prevented the wide acceptance of the universal credit-card plan:

(1) Costs — in a study made by one oil company it was calculated that it would cost 2.5 cents per gallon for the privilege of accepting all credit cards; hence, the major oil companies suggested to their dealers that they not accept "foreign" cards.

(2) Uneducated Public — the public did not understand how universal acceptance worked and they did not like the idea of being billed by a strange company. There was also fear in the industry that a multiplicity of small invoices from many different companies would stir up a self-defeating wave of annoyance.

(3) Location — a third obstacle resulted from the fact that a large majority of stations were so located that they did not draw much transient trade and would not attract additional volume by accepting a "foreign" card. The plan was effective primarily for truck stops located on the main highways.[39]

In 1952, the National Congress of Petroleum Retailers reported unfavorably on universal acceptance of credit cards, giving as its reason the increased costs to the dealers. In 1954, National Credit Card, Incorporated, filed a petition for bankruptcy, charging that "monopoly interests" had sought to scuttle the program.[40] More recent attempts

[38] "Universal Credit Card," *National Petroleum News,* November 19, 1952, p. 29.
[39] *Ibid.*
[40] See "Credit Card Firm Seeks New Life," *National Petroleum News,* March 31, 1954, p. 39; also, "Universal Card Ready," *The Oil and Gas Journal,* June 20, 1960, p. 82.

to promote a single, universally accepted credit card have met with similar obstacles.

With over one hundred million petroleum credit cards presently outstanding, the number of cards will continue to grow at an estimated 15 percent annually. The oil companies continually are expanding the amount and types of purchases which can be made with petroleum company credit cards. The current status and breakdown by issuing companies of oil credit cards are presented in Appendix 4; petroleum company credit-card tie-ins with motels, restaurants, and car-rental agencies are presented in Appendix 5.

5.3. Credit Cards Issued by Retailers

Credit has been advanced by retailers for years as a convenience to customers and as a means of increasing sales volume. Today, approximately two-thirds of all retail sales are made on a credit basis.

The three most common methods of selling on credit are the thirty-day charge account, the revolving charge account, and the installment method. It was mentioned earlier in Chapter 4 that the Federal Reserve Board includes in its definition of "installment credit" revolving charge accounts and any other consumer credit accounts that are paid for in two or more installments. However, from the retailer's point of view it is often helpful to make a distinction between revolving charge accounts and other forms of installment credit. Each of these methods serves different consumer wants.

The credit card is used by many retailers as a device for the extension of thirty-day charge credit and revolving charge credit. The use of these types of credit, however, was popular among retailers before the advent of the credit card. In small towns, the general store often extended credit to local customers simply by recording the amount of purchase and the customer's name. In time some stores issued "credit buttons," and with the advent of the department store came the widespread use of the "charge-a-plate." Today, most large retailers issue a credit card.

The most popular technique for the extension of consumer retail credit is the charge account, which is often conducted with the use of the credit card. Typically, the customer applies for a credit card at the credit department of the merchant's store, and the card permits the holder to make purchases from only that merchant on a ten-to-thirty-day charge basis. The same credit card in most cases will permit the customer to extend the credit period beyond the usual thirty days. A revolving charge account enables the customer to pay a fraction of his total monthly bill and make monthly payments on the balance, usually with a 1.5 percent monthly service charge computed on the outstanding balance.

It is estimated that nearly three-quarters of all American families hold credit cards or have charge accounts. Charge-account credit or service credit is granted not only by retail stores but also by doctors, dentists, automobile garages, plumbers, and by many other professional and service industries. Charge accounts including service credit represent more than two-thirds of all noninstallment credit.

The trend in recent years has been toward the wider adoption of charge accounts for the purchase of shopping goods. Department and wearing apparel specialty stores in particular have been increasing their charge account sales and their issuance of credit cards. The rise of the chain store, the discount house, and the supermarket has brought about new trends in the purchase of convenience goods; today many of these stores are beginning to issue credit cards.

Installment credit is used generally for higher priced purchases, particularly consumer durable goods. Approximately two-thirds of all automobiles and over one-half of all household appliances are sold on an installment basis. Under an installment purchase plan, title to the goods purchased is often retained by the seller until the final payment has been made. Most installment purchases involve a separate contract for each sale. In addition to the signing of a note, the installment sale also involves the signing of a *chattel mortgage* or a *conditional bill of sale*. These legal documents are designed to permit the seller to repossess the goods on which the customer fails to make payments.

The advantages of credit selling to the retailer are numerous. A properly used credit arrangement can reduce substantially consumer price resistance. Recent studies indicate that many families are quite indifferent, within a relatively wide range, to the interest and service charges on credit purchases.[41] It would appear, in fact, that many families today are more concerned with budgeting their credit than their incomes. Not only is a customer likely to purchase a greater quantity of goods when he uses credit instead of cash or checks; he will generally purchase higher quality merchandise, and customers form a habit of buying at the stores with which they have established credit relationships.

Perhaps the greatest advantage of the charge account to the customer is its convenience. There is no need for the customer to anticipate a

[41] See Jean M. Due, "Consumer Knowledge of Instalment Credit Charges," *Journal of Marketing*, October 1955, and F. Thomas Juster, "Consumer Sensitivity to the Price of Credit," *The Journal of Finance*, May 1964.

shopping expedition in terms of the specific items to be purchased and their costs. Another advantage of credit buying to the individual is the greater willingness of retailers to take back or exchange goods if for some reason the consumer decides to return them. Some individuals and companies have indicated that the major disadvantage of credit buying from the consumer's standpoint is that often the easy availability of credit leads a customer to purchase something that is not really needed and may also cause him to overextend his purchases beyond his means to pay for them.

Unfortunately, there are no data available on the number of outstanding credit cards issued by retailers. In fact, the most relevant information available includes installment and noninstallment consumer credit with only major breakdowns for department stores and other retail outlets.[42] These data are presented in Tables 5.1 and 5.2.

It is interesting to note that the department-store industry apparently does not make a profit on its credit activities *per se*. The advantages of increased sales volume and customer loyalty alone must justify a retail store's credit department in most cases. A spokesman for the National Retail Merchants Association stated that

The department store industry, not having the highly leveraged capital structure of a finance company or a bank, and also because of the exceptionally high volume of monthly account activity, purchase, returns, payments, collections and the small amount of most credit sales transactions and payments, has a vastly different cost structure than do other institutions extending credit. Many bank loans, for example, are for a single large fixed sum with fixed periodic payments and thus require far less accounts maintenance and, in fact, no monthly statements. Any failure to pay on time is penalized in many states by a delinquent charge often amounting to as much as 5 or 10% of the monthly payment . . . or under the so-called truth in lending bill's type of mathematics, would constitute an annual rate in excess of 60%.

I cite this because of the fairly widespread misunderstanding about the nature and character of retail credit. In 1963 the NRMA employed Touche, Ross, Bailey and Smart to conduct a study on the cost of credit in retail stores. This study shows quite conclusively that stores in fact do not make money on credit.[43]

A National Retail Merchants Association survey of retail stores indicated that the net cost to department stores for granting credit averaged 2.55 percent of credit sales. The study found that for the stores surveyed all three methods of granting credit (thirty-day charge, revolving charge, and installment sales) were unprofitable. The costs and service-charge income for long-term installment sales were almost equal;

[42] Correspondence with Mr. Sam Flanel, Vice President, National Retail Merchants Association, February 29, 1968.
[43] *Ibid.*

Table 5.1. Consumer Installment Credit for Selected Years (in millions of dollars)

End of Year	Total	Financial Institutions						Retail Outlets					
		Total	Com-mercial Banks	Sales Finance Companies	Credit Unions	Con-sumer Finance[a]	Other[a]	Total	Depart-ment Stores[b]	Furni-ture Stores	Appli-ance Stores	Auto-mobile Dealers	Other
1939	4,503	3,065	1,079	1,197	132	—	657	1,438	354	439	183	123	339
1941	6,085	4,480	1,726	1,797	198	—	759	1,605	320	496	206	188	395
1945	2,462	1,776	745	300	102	—	629	686	131	240	17	28	270
1960	42,832	37,218	16,672	11,472	3,923	3,670	1,481	5,615	2,414	1,107	333	359	1,402
1961	43,527	37,935	17,008	11,273	4,330	3,779	1,525	5,595	2,421	1,058	293	342	1,481
1962	48,034	41,782	19,005	12,194	4,902	4,131	1,505	6,252	3,013	1,073	294	345	1,527
1963	54,158	47,405	22,023	13,523	5,622	4,590	1,647	6,753	3,427	1,086	287	328	1,625
1964	60,548	53,141	25,094	14,762	6,458	5,078	1,749	7,407	3,922	1,152	286	370	1,677
1965	68,565	60,273	29,173	16,138	7,512	5,606	1,844	8,292	4,488	1,235	302	447	1,820
1966	74,656	65,565	32,155	16,936	8,549	6,014	1,911	9,091	n.a.	n.a.	n.a.	490	n.a.

[a] Consumer finance companies included with "other" financial institutions until 1950.
[b] Includes mail-order houses.
Source: Federal Reserve Bulletin, January 1968.

Table 5.2.   Consumer Noninstallment Credit for Selected Years (in millions of dollars).

| End of Year | Total | Single-Payment Loans | | Charge Accounts | | Credit Cards[b] | Service Credit |
		Commercial Banks	Other Financial Institutions	Department Stores[a]	Other Retail Outlets		
1939	2,719	625	162	236	1,178	—	518
1941	3,087	698	152	275	1,370	—	597
1945	3,203	674	72	290	1,322	—	845
1960	13,196	3,884	623	941	3,952	436	3,360
1961	14,151	4,413	723	948	3,907	469	3,691
1962	15,130	4,690	766	927	4,252	505	3,990
1963	16,303	5,205	912	895	4,456	520	4,315
1964	17,894	5,950	1,004	909	4,756	635	4,640
1965	19,319	6,587	1,095	968	5,055	723	4,891
1966	20,130	6,714	1,130	n.a.	n.a.	874	5,142

[a] Includes mail-order houses.
[b] Service-station and miscellaneous credit-card accounts and home-heating oil accounts.
Source: *Federal Reserve Bulletin*, January 1968.

revolving charge accounts were found to be the next most costly, and the thirty-day account was the most costly. For small stores in the survey, none of the three types of accounts yielded revenues to exceed 65 percent of the costs of extending the credit. The poorer results for small stores were attributed to a smaller sales volume and an inability to spread fixed credit costs over a large volume of transactions.[44]

In order to compete effectively in today's markets, it has become almost a necessity for the retail merchant to offer some forms of credit. Credit is costly to the retailer, but he is faced with the necessity of meeting competition and maintaining an adequate sales volume. The dilemma faced by the retailer has been stated, "Indeed, it would seem that the average department store could enhance its profits by eliminating the credit function — if it could maintain the same sales volume." [45]

[44] See "Credit Costs — and Costs Even More for Smaller Stores," *Stores*, March 1965, p. 36.
[45] *Ibid.*, p. 37.

Bank credit cards and preauthorized payments are relatively new phenomena in payment media systems. Both of these innovations have become increasingly important since early 1965. These are the two most significant developments in debt settlement that have given rise to speculations of a future "cashless-checkless" society.

6.1. Bank Credit Cards

Bank credit cards are not significantly different from other types of credit cards, except that they are issued by banks and tend to be used primarily in the trading area which is served by the issuing bank. Having its genesis in the early 1950s, the bank credit card began to spread across the country with amazing rapidity in the mid-1960s. Bank credit cards are issued to individuals free of charge and may be used to make purchases at a large variety of participating merchants. Not only is the bank credit card used for purchases, it has become a convenient and relatively inexpensive vehicle for banks to extend short-term consumer credit.

6.1.1. The Development of Commercial Bank Credit Cards. The first entrance into the bank credit-card field was made by the Franklin National Bank of New York in 1952. The general purposes for engaging in "charge-account banking" were (1) to provide a new service for the retail merchants in areas where Franklin had branches or planned to establish branches; (2) to increase purchasing convenience for existing bank customers and to attract new accounts; (3) to attract new deposits, both consumer and merchant; and (4) to provide an additional source of earnings for the bank. Since approximately 1955, Franklin's charge account department has been operating profitably, and the bank's management feels that its credit-card activities have accomplished its purposes.[1]

The basic system that Franklin installed originally is still in operation today. Essentially the credit-card system works as follows: Customers are issued a Franklin National Bank credit card that may be used instead of checks or cash in transactions with local merchants who

[1] Correspondence with Mr. Steven A. Vanden Bergh, Vice President, Franklin National Bank, New York, July 31, 1967.

subscribe to the arrangement. When making a purchase, the customer presents his credit card to the salesman. The salesman fills out a charge-account sales ticket indicating a description of the merchandise, the unit cost, and the total amount of the charge. The card and the sales ticket are inserted in an imprinter, which imprints the customer's name and account number and the dealer's name, address, and account number. The customer signs his name and receives a copy of the sales ticket. Every several days the merchant mails in his "deposit" of sales drafts. The bank credits the merchant's account for the total amount of charges less a discount which ranges from 5 percent to 2 percent. The standard, original discount is 5 percent; however, the amount of discount is scaled downward based on the merchant's semi-annual average sale and his semiannual sales volume.

At the end of the month the credit-card holder receives a statement showing all the details of his payments and charges. If the customer pays his account in full within thirty days, there is no charge, or if he elects, the account may be spread over a period of months. The service charge for the extension of credit beyond thirty days is 1.5 percent per month on the outstanding balance.[2] In providing a credit card, the bank has two sources of revenue: the merchant discount and the interest charges on deferred-payment accounts.

Two additional features of the Franklin credit-card plan include its telephone authorization procedure and its "piggyback" instant account. If when a customer's purchase exceeds the authorized limit, the salesman is instructed to telephone the bank by a special number depending upon the first letter of the customer's last name, giving the name of the store, the customer's name and address, the total amount of the sale, and the credit-card account number. If authorization is advanced, an additional code number is placed on the sales ticket, and the transaction is consummated.

The "piggyback" instant account enables a customer who does not have a Franklin credit card to make a credit purchase up to fifty dollars. If the customer has an unexpired national credit card, a major local department store credit card, or another local bank credit card he may fill out and sign a Franklin credit-card application provided by the merchant and charge his purchase on a temporary account number which the salesman obtains from the bank via a special telephone number.

In September 1952, the First National Bank and Trust Company of Kalamazoo, Michigan, entered the charge account-banking field. This

---

[2] The service charge is scaled downward on balances in excess of five hundred dollars.

was the first bank credit-card plan in the Midwest and the second in the United States, following the lead of Franklin National. The primary motivation for offering a credit card was to open a new avenue for earnings for the bank.[3] The bank's management also felt that it would gain many collateral benefits, such as increased demand deposits and more customer usage of other bank services. A spokesman for the bank stated that these benefits have been realized. "Not only has the charge plan been extremely profitable (one of the highest yields on invested funds in the bank) but we have gained many customers, both merchant and individual." [4]

Initially, First National offered only a thirty-day charge plan with no extended terms, making the only source of revenue for the bank the merchant discount. In 1957, the bank installed the option account, which allows the customer to pay one-fourth of his balance and carry the remainder for a charge of 1 percent per month on the unpaid balance. Today, the repayment terms have been extended to permit the payment of one-twentieth of the original balance and the extension of the remainder on a deferred-payment basis.

In the late 1950s several of the country's largest banks began to implement credit-card systems. Operationally these plans were no different from Franklin National's and First National's; however, the reasons for offering credit cards were much more influenced by competitive forces and technological advances made during the 1950s. The large California banks were the primary leaders in the adaptation of electronic data-processing technology to payment media systems. Today, the San Francisco Federal Reserve District, which includes all of the West Coast states, holds over one-third of the outstanding credit in all bank-credit plans. It will be useful to analyze the major economic and institutional developments in California banking during the period of the 1950s and early 1960s.

6.1.2. Trends Toward Bank Credit-Card Development in California. During the rapid industrial and economic expansion after World War II, California experienced a greater than average growth in population, of industrialization, and in demand-deposit balances. The number of demand-deposit accounts increased from 3.1 million in 1946 to 5.6 million in 1962, and during the early postwar years the average-size balance declined. By 1966, the volume of checks passing through Cali-

[3] Duncan G. Carter, "Today's Decisions for Progress and Profit in Credit Card Banking," Address before the Annual Bank Operations — NABAC Conference, April 5, 1967.
[4] Correspondence with Mr. Duncan G. Carter, Assistant Vice President and Manager of Charge Account Service, First National Bank and Trust Company of Kalamazoo, Michigan, July 20, 1967.

fornia banks was double the 1946 volume. The banks were required to process a greater volume of checks per dollar of demand deposits held, and they were put under considerable pressure to acquire additional earnings per dollar of assets and to reduce the costs of handling the increased volume of checks.[5] According to a survey conducted by the Federal Reserve Bank of Boston, over one-half of a bank's operating expenses other than interest on time deposits is allocable to its payments function.[6]

During this same period banks experienced growing staffing problems. Over a quarter of a million new jobs opened (other than at the officer level) in banks across the country during 1946–1963, and more than one of every eight was in California. In the bookkeeping and check-collection positions there was an annual turnover rate in excess of 100 percent. In an attempt to offset the growing "cost squeeze," banks sought new markets for services and methods for cutting operating costs. The development of electronic data processing and computer technology presented an opportunity for innovation in payment media systems. Richard Towey states:

The rising postwar check volume, with the attendant cost pressures and staffing problems, has been largely responsible for the recent adaptation of high speed electronic data processing equipment to payments processing, in which the large California banks have been among the national leaders. The speed of response [adaptation of electronic data processing] . . . may suggest also that at least a segment of the banking industry has a hitherto little-suspected propensity to innovate. It may be only that opportunities for innovation in the payments field were rather limited before the advent of automation.[7]

The primary use of computers and related data-processing equipment by the banks has been in demand-deposit bookkeeping. However, once this process has been automated, a bank has typically sought new profitable applications of its computer capabilities. In many cases due to excess computer capacity, banks have attempted to broaden their range of profitable customer services related to the making of payments. Such services now offered include payroll preparation, including employee-account deposits and account reconciliation; lock-box services; automatic funds transfers to savings and Christmas Club accounts; automatic payment of reoccurring bills, such as utility and insurance premium payments; and credit cards.

[5] See Richard E. Towey, "An Evaluation of the Payments Mechanism in California, 1946–1975," in Hyman P. Minsky, *California Banking in a Growing Economy: 1946–1975* (Berkeley: Institute of Business and Economic Research, University of California, 1965), pp. 331–356.
[6] Federal Reserve Bank of Boston, *Functional Cost Analysis,* 1961 and 1962.
[7] Towey, in Minsky, *California Banking,* p. 340.

6.1.3. BankAmericard. The major bank credit card in California and the nation is the BankAmericard, issued by the country's largest bank, the Bank of America. According to a spokesman for the bank, the Bank of America first became interested in credit cards about 1946.[8] However, it was thought that economic conditions at that time were not conducive to launching such a program, and plans were postponed until 1951. But the complexities of financing the Korean War delayed serious research until 1955, when plans were formed to conduct a market test of the credit card in the city of Fresno. Initial success in Fresno led to an expansion of credit-card activities into the cities of Bakersfield, Sacramento, Los Angeles, and San Francisco, and in October 1959 the decision was reached to expand the program throughout the entire state of California.

In order to implement rapidly a statewide program, the Bank of America issued about 2,500,000 cards to customers who were known to be good credit risks as a result of previous borrowing experience with the bank. Many people received cards who did not want a BankAmericard; for this and other reasons, by the end of 1960 cancellations reduced the number of card holders to about 1,500,000. Since that time, however, the total number of cardholders has surpassed the original number, and merchant membership is now approximately 74,000 within the state of California. According to the Bank of America, its dollar volume of credit-card sales has shown an increase of 30 to 35 percent annually for the last three years. In 1966, $228,000,000 in goods and services were purchased with BankAmericards in California. In mid-July 1967, the bank estimated its 1967 California sales to be $275,000,000 to $280,000,000;[9] however, in January 1968, the Bank of America reported California sales with BankAmericards were $335,-100,000, an increase of about 75 percent over the 1966 level.[10]

The merchants honoring BankAmericards are required to maintain deposit accounts with the bank, into which their sales drafts less discount must be deposited. When sales drafts are delivered to the bank, the merchant receives immediate credit. A flat discount rate is charged on all sales and is deducted by the bank at the time the merchant's account is credited. The discount rate is determined by the type of business indicated in Table 6.1. Other costs to the merchant include a twenty-five dollar "sign-up fee" and a five-dollar annual rental fee on each imprinter which the bank supplies.

[8] Correspondence with Mr. Charles A. Brackenbury, Coordinator of Sales and Services, BankAmericard Center, Pasadena, California, July 17, 1967.
[9] *Ibid.*
[10] "Bank of America Says Use of Its Credit Card Rose in '67," *The Wall Street Journal,* January 10, 1968, p. 22.

Table 6.1. BankAmericard Merchant Discount Rates—1968.

5%	4%	3%
Service stations	Hotels	All
Food and liquor stores	Motels	others
Drug and variety stores	Restaurants	
Laundries and cleaners	Taverns	

Source: *BankAmericard Member Operating Guide.*

The cardholder is billed monthly on a computer cycle billing arrangement. The monthly statement may be paid in full within twenty-five days without charge, or the cardholder may elect to pay as little as 5 percent of the total bill and defer the balance which is subject to a 1.5 percent per month service charge. The cardholder's purchases have the same legal status as if cash had been paid since title to the article purchased passes from seller to buyer upon delivery; no repossession rights are retained by the retailer or the bank.

Several techniques are used by the bank to prevent misuse of its credit cards. First, there are two types of BankAmericards—starred and unstarred, and a dollar floor limit has been set for each type of card. The starred card has a single-purchase limit of one hundred dollars and a "fundamental credit limit" of five hundred dollars; the unstarred card's limits are fifty dollars and three hundred and fifty dollars, respectively. Approval to exceed these limits may be obtained by telephoning the nearest BankAmericard center. Second, the bank's computers are programed to alert the bank when a cardholder approaches his credit limit. Third, the computer also warns the bank when a card is used three times in any one day for three purchases totaling one hundred dollars or more. Fourth, as a check against fraudulent usage and delinquency, BankAmericards expire every six months.[11]

In order to give an added convenience to its customers and to obtain another source of income for the bank, the Bank of America allows a cardholder to obtain an immediate cash loan up to $350 at any branch of the bank merely by presenting his BankAmericard. The repayment schedule and service charges (interest rate) on cash advances are the same as for deferred-charge balances, except that an additional 4 percent service charge is levied on the amount of the loan no matter when it is repaid. For example, if a cardholder receives a one-hundred-dollar cash advance, his bill will read $104. If he pays within twenty-five

[11] See "The Charge-It Plan that Really Took Off," *Business Week*, February 2, 1965, p. 58.

days after receiving his statement, there is no additional charge. If he pays his bill immediately approximately twenty-five days after making his loan, the bank receives an effective rate of interest on an annual basis of approximately 58 percent.[12]

The Bank of America has extended its credit-card services to other states through franchise agreements with other banks. As of mid-1967 there were franchise banks in Hawaii, Washington, Oregon, Idaho, Utah, Colorado, Texas, Tennessee, Ohio, North Carolina, Pennsylvania, and Massachusetts. BankAmericard also has reciprocal arrangements with Barclays Bank Limited, authorized throughout the United Kingdom. At the end of 1967, it was estimated that there were over five million BankAmericard holders, and this number was expected to increase to eight million by the end of 1968.

To the Bank of America its credit-card activities have multiple advantages. Although specific data are not available, the return on investment in the bank's credit-card operations would appear to be relatively high. The two major sources of income are interest and service charges on preauthorized lines of credit to cardholders and the merchant discount. The stated service charge on deferred payments is 1.5 percent per month or the equivalent of 18 percent per year. Generally banks rarely break even on personal loans of less than $350, but by shifting these loans over to BankAmericard, the bank saves credit-checking costs, paperwork, and employee time. The effective rate of return which the bank can realize on loans which are repaid within twenty-five days was discussed earlier in this chapter.

A merchant discount of 5 percent also represents a high yield on loaned funds. For example, suppose that the bank receives a sales ticket from a participating retailer for one hundred dollars. The bank credits the retailer's demand-deposit account for $95 and bills the cardholder for the full amount. If the cardholder pays his bill within twenty-five days after making the purchase, the bank in effect has made a $95 loan to the merchant for twenty-five days for a charge of five dollars. Because the sales ticket was discounted, the effective interest yield is close to 5.3 percent for twenty-five days or over 77 percent on an annual basis.

Not only does the bank receive a substantial amount of advertising benefits by having its credit cards in the hands of millions of customers, but merchants also very willingly display the bank's window decals, outdoor signs, wall signs, and BankAmericard application forms. The bank also claims that its credit card has attracted new customers who

[12] The use of $100 for 25 days at a cost of 4% or $4 is equal to $4 times (365 ÷ 25), or $58.40, which is 58.4% of $100.

open accounts and use other bank services. Similarly, a commercial account is opened automatically for merchants who join the credit-card plan. According to a BankAmericard spokesman, there are over 125,000 business locations to which cardholders have access. Each location would need to rent a minimum of one imprinter, and many would need several. Assuming just one imprinter per business location at a five-dollar annual rental fee, yearly revenues from imprinters alone would be $625,000. Also, assuming that there were about one hundred thousand separate businesses which paid an initial "sign-up" fee of twenty-five dollars, this amount plus one year's imprinter rental fees would produce over three million dollars in revenue before a single credit-card charge or cash advance was made.

6.1.4. The Widespread Issuance of Bank Credit Cards. The profit potential and collateral benefits of credit cards have enticed many banks since early 1965 to enter the charge-account banking field either by issuing their own cards, participating in joint bank-card programs, or by acquiring an existing credit-card company. In some cases banks have taken more than one approach to entering the credit-card business and have offered multiple card plans to serve different markets. In 1965, particular impetus was given to the expansion of national banks into the credit-card field by the Comptroller of the Currency, James Saxon. Previously the Banking Act of 1933 generally had barred nationally chartered banks from holding common stock except in the liquidation of collateralized loans. Saxon's liberal interpretation of the law stated that the law was

"not to be construed as denying to a national bank the power to own corporate stock . . . when such ownership is a proper incident to banking. The precise scope of this incidental power has never been defined, nor should it be," and he concluded that questions of this nature were "to be determined by this office in the light of the development of banking and banking services."

Financial World interpreted Mr. Saxon's remarks saying Mr. Saxon seemed to be saying that the law is what he says it is. Hence, as long as he will permit them, national banks are going to get into the credit card business.[13]

During the period of the early 1960s several of the nation's larger banks began issuing credit cards. Such banks included Marine Midland Trust of Western New York, Mellon National Bank and Trust Company, Pittsburgh National Bank, Valley National Bank of Arizona, the Citizens and Southern National Bank (Atlanta), and the Bank of Hawaii.[14] Since 1965, hundreds of banks have either initiated their own

[13] "Credit Card Kaleidoscope," *Financial World,* December 15, 1965, p. 14.
[14] Actually one of the first large banks to offer credit cards was the Chase Manhattan Bank of New York, at the time the second largest bank in the

card programs or have agreed to participate in licensee or joint-bank credit-card arrangements.

In 1967, the Federal Reserve System began expressing concern over the proliferation of bank credit cards. For example, in Chicago there were scores of instances in which the large-scale mailing of unsolicited bank credit cards resulted in cards being stolen before they reached the addressee. One news report stated:

In Illinois, a [bank] credit card is addressed to a woman in Peoria four months after her death. Another is mailed to a two-year-old infant.

It is all part of the instant money game. Americans have been playing it for well over a decade under the auspices of such national organizations as American Express and Diners' Club and local charge-a-plate.

But banks have begun invading the field in droves over the past year, and their headlong rush to meet each other's competition is raising eyebrows of federal and state regulators.[15]

Competitive pressures have forced many banks to cooperate in joint-bank credit-card ventures. In 1966, five banks (Continental Illinois National Bank and Trust Company, Central National Bank in Chicago, The First National Bank of Chicago, Harris Trust and Savings Bank, and the Pullman Bank and Trust Company) organized the Midwest Bank Card System. By mid-1967, the system had expanded to include more than thirteen card-issuing banks in Illinois, Indiana, Michigan, Wisconsin, and Kentucky, with sixty thousand retailers honoring cards held by six million families.[16]

In California four major banks (Bank of California, Crocker Citizens National Bank, United California Bank, and Wells Fargo Bank) organized the California Bankcard Association. By early 1967, sixty-two banks in California agreed to participate in the clearinghouse plan. To ensure a nationwide market the Association quickly arranged an agreement with Inter-bank Card, a clearing house affiliated with over two hundred banks (including Buffalo's Marine Midland, Pittsburgh's Mellon National, and Phoenix's Valley National Bank).

The California Bankcard Association operates as a nonprofit clear-

country. Shortly after being introduced, however, the credit card was found too unprofitable, and it was discontinued. Little information is available on why the bank's attempt was unsuccessful. One spokesman for the bank claimed the card failed because cardholders were charged only 1 percent per month on deferred balances. See "Charge Accounts at the Chase," *Business Week*, October 25, 1958, p. 96; and "Throwing in the Sponge," *Forbes*, February 1, 1962, p. 60.

[15] "US 'Instant Money Game' Increasingly 'Played' Today," (UPI), *Austin American Statesman*, November 5, 1967, p. A17. Also see, "Careless Issuance of Credit Cards by Banks Stirs Federal Reserve Worry over Risks," *The Wall Street Journal*, August 21, 1967, p. 2.

[16] "Credit," *Time*, April 21, 1967, p. 91.

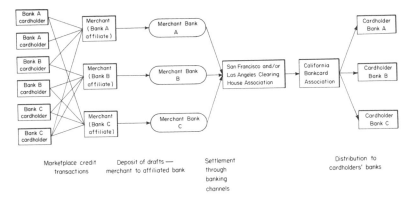

Figure 6.1. Operational configuration of the California Bankcard Association. Flow of Sales Drafts. (Source: Information Sciences Associates.)

inghouse for its member banks. In the marketplace, any member bank's cardholders may transact credit sales with merchants affiliated with any member bank. The merchants deposit their sales drafts with their affiliated banks, at which time they receive credit less a discount. The members process all of the sales drafts at par for payment at the City Collection Department of the San Francisco and/or Los Angeles Clearing House Association. At the California Bankcard Association, the drafts are sorted and totaled by the cardholders' banks, which pay for the drafts presented, and the sales drafts are returned eventually to the cardholders with their monthly statements.[17] Figure 6.1 shows the operational configuration of the California Bankcard Association.

A fully operational, large-scale credit-card organization offers several advantages to its members. Bank credit cards can be very profitable, but a large volume of card transactions is required to support the credit balances and merchant discounts to produce sufficient interest income. Start-up costs are great, fixed costs are high, and typically a bank must be prepared to absorb a loss on its card operations for the first two to five years. As merchant discounts have been driven down by competition in many areas, conditions are becoming more difficult for banks to reach the break-even point. Cooperative plans permit the participating banks to share heavy start-up costs and the high credit risks of a mass distribution of cards.

[17] *A Summary of the Feasibility Determination and Implementation Plan Report for a Common Bank Credit Card Plan* (Prepared for Bank of California, N. A., Croker Citizens National Bank, United California Bank, and Wells Fargo Bank by Information Sciences Associates, Cherry Hill, New Jersey), September 19, 1966.

6.1.5. The Current Status of Bank Credit Cards. Statistics on bank credit cards are rather scanty, and because the credit-card field is growing so rapidly, collected data are quickly outdated. Some information was made available by the April 27, 1967, Call Reports of the three federal bank-regulatory agencies. As of that date, $809 million in credit was outstanding at the 627 banks which offered some kind of credit plan. At that time there were probably more than 627 banks involved with credit cards, since in many areas correspondent banks offer cards and service merchants but do not carry any credit balances. In fact, in January 1968 it was reported that about 1,400 commercial banks were offering some sort of credit card.[18]

Unfortunately in the statistics collected by the Call Reports there was no distinction made between bank credit-card plans and bank check-credit plans.[19] The $809 million represented approximately one-fifth of an estimated total of five billion dollars outstanding for all types of consumer credit-card plans. Of the 627 banks reporting credit-card or check-credit plans, 372 were national banks, 90 were state bank members of the Federal Reserve System, and 165 were insured non-member banks. The major areas where these banks were located were the East, West Coast, and Midwest. The largest number of banks in any Federal Reserve district was 138 in the Chicago District; however, in terms of dollar volume the largest amount of credit outstanding was reported in the San Francisco Federal Reserve District.

Most credit-card and check-credit plans are operated by medium- to large-size banks. Over one-third of the banks reporting in April 1967 had total deposits of more than one hundred million dollars. Tables 6.2 and 6.3 contain the results of the statistical tabulations.

6.2. Bank Preauthorized Payments

Bank preauthorized-payment plans involve the automatic debiting and/or crediting of bank depository accounts in accordance with the

---

[18] "The Other Side of the Credit Card," *Finance*, January 1968, p. 13.

[19] Check-credit plans (bankcard checks) began developing rapidly across the country at about the same time as bank credit-card systems. These "credit checks" are issued by banks and are very similar to travelers' checks, except they are not paid for in advance. The arrangement operates like an overdraft or line-of-credit agreement. A customer may obtain "credit checks," use them to make purchases, and pay for them with interest over several months' time.

"Credit check" plans have been implemented by many banks that have not started credit-card programs, particularly in areas where a competing bank has initiated a credit card. In some ways the "credit check" can compete with the credit card. The signed bank draft is acceptable almost anywhere, and the credit card must be presented to a participating merchant. However, in a local market area the credit card offers much greater convenience to the bank customer.

Table 6.2. Bank Credit Cards and Check Credit: Total Credit Outstanding as of April 25, 1967 (amounts in millions of dollars).

Federal Reserve District	National Banks		State Member Banks		State Nonmember Banks		All Banks	
	No. of Banks	Total Credit	No. of Banks	Total Credit	No. of Banks	Total Credit	No. of Banks	Total Credit
1. Boston	28	44	11	13	8	2	47	59
2. New York	34	61	25	46	11	9	70	116
3. Philadelphia	23	20	7	40	9	6	39	66
4. Cleveland	27	54	1	a	8	1	36	55
5. Richmond	16	18	5	12	7	2	28	31
6. Atlanta	51	40	7	3	23	5	81	48
7. Chicago	78	95	12	18	48	9	138	122
8. St. Louis	22	10	6	2	17	2	45	13
9. Minneapolis	15	4	1	a	6	a	22	4
10. Kansas City	29	10	6	1	5	a	40	12
11. Dallas	19	3	3	2	11	5	33	10
12. San Francisco	30	248	6	13	12	11	48	272
Total	372	607	90	150	165	52	627	809

a Less than $500,000.
Source: Federal Reserve Board of Governors.

prior authorization of the account holder. Typical of such arrangements are the automatic debiting of customers' reoccurring payments such as utility bills, insurance premiums, rent, mortgage payments; and the automatic crediting of accounts for payroll deposits, pension deposits, and rental income. Although the concept of preauthorized payments is not new, it was not until recent developments in automation technology that the widespread implementation of preauthorized payments appeared to be realistically feasible to the banking community. For purposes of discussion, preauthorized payments will be divided into two major areas: preauthorized debit plans and preauthorized credit plans.

6.2.1. Preauthorized Debit Plans. As might be expected, in the latter 1950s preauthorized payment plans were given serious attention by banks that had newly acquired computer and electronic data-processing capabilities. Before this time preauthorized payments were not encouraged by the banks. Many banks offered "Sav-O-Magic" and "Christmas Club" accounts, which required manual processing. "Automatic" savings plans, for example, required an individual to prepare tickets debiting a customer's checking account and crediting his savings ac-

Table 6.3.   Distribution of Insured Commercial Banks Reporting Credit-Card and Check-Credit Plans April 25, 1967.

By Size of Bank

Amount of Deposits (millions of dollars)	Number of Banks
Under 5	27
5–10	58
10–25	113
25–50	103
50–100	98
100–500	159
500–1,000	36
Over 1,000	33
	627

By Amount of Credit Outstanding

Amount of Credit (thousands of dollars)	Number of Banks
Under 25	194
25–50	50
50–100	71
100–250	87
250–500	61
500–1,000	65
1,000–10,000	77
Over 10,000	22
	627

Source: Federal Reserve Board of Governors.

count. Generally, these manual transfers were costly and inconvenient for the bank.

In the early 1960s one bank that studied the feasibility of establishing a computerized automatic transfer file for handling existing preauthorized payments found that such a system would be justified from a cost-reduction standpoint for Christmas Club accounts alone. A spokesman for that bank stated:

Our studies relating to Xmas Club costs and profitability prior to establishment of our [computerized] Transfer File indicated that the only profitable clubs were those of $500. — or more. Since the implementation of the preauthorized Debit/Credit File, which incidentally, has eliminated all coupon books and all physical entries on transfers, we find our only unprofitable Automatic Transfer Xmas Club to be the

$50. — club, and this is for the first year only. Also, of some significance, clubs carried on a nonautomatic basis show approximately 60% completion. Automatic Transfer Clubs boast a 95% completion factor.[20]

In addition to Christmas Club and automatic savings accounts, banks with computer equipment have begun using automatic funds-transfers for installment-loan customers, who have their payments deducted from demand-deposit accounts automatically. Two other major areas where customers' accounts are debited automatically are for the payment of insurance premiums and utility bills.

PREAUTHORIZED INSURANCE PAYMENTS. As late as ten years ago, preauthorized insurance drafts were almost universally regarded as a bane by the banking community. Encouragement for preauthorization was given by the insurance industry, but most banks refused to enter this area. One banker summarized the objections of his industry as follows:

A. Operational Objections
 1. Fear of nonconformity to check format standards
 2. Need to refer to authorization files
 3. Need to advise depositors of charges to their accounts
 4. Fear of an increase in forgery losses
 5. Fear that the paying process would become more cumbersome and costly
 6. Fear of an increase in overdrafts and returned items
B. Adverse Public Relations
 1. Fear that discretion by the bank over what companies and depositors would be allowed to participate would be regarded as discrimination by the public
 2. Fear that an error by the bank might result in a policy lapse
C. Philosophical
 1. A feeling that it is fundamentally wrong for a depositor to lose control over his account
 2. Preauthorization of insurance drafts might spread to other areas and compound problems[21]

Demands by the insurance industry led many banks to participate reluctantly in preauthorized insurance draft plans. For several years these banks feared the possible spread of the preauthorized payment technique to areas other than the insurance field. Today, many banks are examining ways to make the use of preauthorization even more widespread. Although no data are available currently on the extent of

[20] George E. Lowther, Assistant Vice President, Wells Fargo Bank, San Francisco, California. Presentation before The American Bankers Association's Preauthorized Payments Workshop, New Orleans, Louisiana, January 25–26, 1968.
[21] Richard V. Banks, Vice President, First National City Bank, New York, New York. Presentation before The American Bankers Association's Preauthorized Payments Workshop, New Orleans, Louisiana, January 25–26, 1968.

use of preauthorized debit plans, some insight into this rapidly growing field may be gained by examining the experience of one of the
nation's largest banks.

The First National City Bank of New York, like most other banks,
looked upon preauthorized insurance drafts with considerable sus-
picion. In the mid-1950s, Citibank entered the preauthorization area on
a limited basis. In addition to the bank's rigid requirements on indem-
nification and draft formats, the company involved had to be in the
insurance business and had to be a depositor in the bank. The individual customer requesting the preauthorized service had to be a regular
checking-account customer. In 1956, Citibank participated with three
insurance companies. Favorable results with these companies led the
bank to change its policies.

Today, the First National City Bank freely accepts preauthorization
requests from all checking-account depositors, provided that (1) the company authorized to draft on the account furnishes the bank a suitable
indemnity agreement (there is no longer an industry requirement);
(2) the company has the financial capacity to make good on its indemnity undertaking; and (3) the format of the draft conforms to
existing standards.[22]

By 1964, Citibank was cooperating in preauthorized draft plans with
70 companies and had a rapidly growing depositor list. Today, the
bank has over 150 companies on its approved list, including a half
dozen mutual funds. The bank pays about sixteen thousand drafts
monthly and is the depository for over one hundred thousand drafts
monthly.

A vice-president of the bank has stated that managements' original
fears have not materialized, and that the bank has not had any problems of consequence. He elaborated by saying,

The format fear, of course, ended early as the companies demonstrated
they could and would conform to banking standards. In fact, many
of the drafts deposited with us today are completely MICR encoded,
including amount which makes them easier to handle.

The paying process has not proven to be more cumbersome or costly.
We don't check authorization and we don't send out debit advices. And
we have had no forgery losses.

The policy lapse problem also has not materialized. . . . In case of
actual loss due to lapse, the bank is protected by the indemnity. . . .

The old philosophical objections cannot really be examined in the
light of experience; however, it appears that with the passage of time,
they have dimmed. Preauthorization does not imply or result in any
loss of control by a depositor over his account. It may even encourage
better record keeping and better budgeting.[23]

[22] *Ibid.*
[23] *Ibid.*

CHECKLESS UTILITY-PAYMENT SERVICES. A typical checkless utility-payment service is the one offered by the First National Bank of Canton, Canton, Ohio. The system operates as follows: The bank sought an agreement with the two major electric and gas utilities in its market area. Initial discussions led to a six-month trial program and eventually to a permanent system. A bank customer signs a form which authorizes the bank to charge his checking account for the amount of his electric and/or gas bill. The utility company is notified and incorporates the customer's bank account number into its records. Each day the utility companies make a "deposit" of their customers' bills, and the bills are treated by the bank in exactly the same manner as if a deposit by check or currency had been made. The bills follow the same processing procedure as a regular deposit.

Because the utilities employ punched-card bills, as many businesses are now doing, it is a fairly simple matter for the bank to convert the bills to its computer records. After computer processing through the bank's demand-deposit system, the bills are canceled and placed in the canceled-check files. The paid bill is mailed to the customer along with his canceled checks and checking-account statement.[24]

Although no specific data are available, the most direct benefit to the bank appears to be a processing-cost savings in its payment functions. In fact, the entire processing system for utility bills is the same as for checks, except that the bank is handling a punched-card bill instead of a magnetically encoded check. The bank's customers are charged the same as if they had written checks to pay their bills. The First National Bank of Canton has proposed that it handle completely a utility's accounts receivable; although it is not performing this service at the present time, other banks have entered this area.

Preauthorized debit plans involve a relationship among a company, the customer, and a bank. The advantages and disadvantages of preauthorization to each of these sectors may be summarized as follows:

Companies

A. Advantages

1. Most companies mail bills in envelopes and provide return envelopes, so the company saves the cost of both envelopes and outgoing postage.
2. Cost savings are realized by a reduction in clerical effort and processing time for checks and cash.
3. The company has the use of collections more quickly and saves the cost of delinquent reminders.

[24] Carl W. Cantor, Vice President, First National Bank of Canton, Canton, Ohio. Presentation before The American Bankers Association's Preauthorized Payments Workshop, New Orleans, Louisiana, January 25–26, 1968.

B. Disadvantages

1. The company gives up a low-cost method of distributing promotional and public relations material with its regular billings.
2. Authorization must be obtained by the company from their customers to draw on their checking accounts.
3. In almost all cases the company will have to maintain customers who wish to be billed in the traditional manner, making it impossible for the company to eliminate its billings altogether.

Customers

A. Advantages

1. The customers save time and the postage costs for mailing checks to the company.
2. All record keeping is done by the company and the bank.
3. The customer is assured that his remittance will be made on time, which prevents him from incurring penalty charges and enables him to maintain a satisfactory credit record.

B. Disadvantages

1. The customer cannot extend payment until or past the due date, which makes it impossible for him to take full advantage of the credit period and the check float.
2. The customer loses control of his funds on the date payment is made by the bank.
3. The customer cannot easily refuse or delay payment because he is dissatisfied with his service or for some other reason.

Banks

A. Advantages

1. Normally the processing costs of preauthorized payments are less than for checks.
2. Some banks provide magnetic encoding services and offer to handle the entire billing and collecting functions of a company for a fee.
3. Most preauthorized payments are handled on a fully indemnified basis.
4. Business firms and customers may be encouraged to maintain larger deposits and use other bank services.

B. Disadvantages

1. If a preauthorized draft is used, the cost is substantially the same as for a check.
2. The bank incurs the cost of the administration of authorizations.
3. Company-authorized deposits tend to peak in volume on the first and fifteenth of each month.

6.2.2. Preauthorized Credit Plans. "Preauthorized credit plans" refers to the automatic flow of funds or credits into bank depository accounts.

Typical of such arrangements are the automatic payroll deposit programs, prearranged dividend or interest deposits, Social Security or other pension deposits, and the automatic crediting of rental income. To date, the most popular of these services has been the automatic payroll-deposit program.

A number of banks are expanding into preauthorized credit plans; however, many banks have not initiated programs as rapidly as might be expected. One bank executive indicated that the banking industry has developed a confused viewpoint on the objectives of preauthorized credit plans. He stated, "There appears to be an unenlightened sponsorship of this new service with only hazy ideas about objectives or benefits to either their bank or the industry." [25] He claims that the unsettled question is whether (1) banks should view preauthorized-payment plans as new service offerings from which the bank can enjoy "near-term" marketing or profit improvements, or (2) banks should regard these plans as methods of streamlining traditional money-transfer procedures with more remote gains to individual banks and the industry stemming from fewer checks in the economy and hence lowered operating costs.

Even though the ultimate advantages of preauthorized credit plans may fall more heavily in one or the other areas already mentioned, it appears only logical that the many banks which have established and offer a preauthorized program have done so with the primary motivation of obtaining "near-term" marketing and profit benefits. And the banks which have not implemented such programs have been restrained due to the lack of a market or computer capabilities, or have not anticipated sufficient benefits occurring to their individual banks.

The potential utilization of preauthorized credit plans appears almost limitless. With a national labor force of about seventy-five million people having an average pay frequency somewhere between thirty-five and forty times per year, payroll-deposit plans alone could eliminate over three billion checks annually. At the present time, the cost to the banking system on the average for processing three billion checks is close to $450,000,000.

For a large bank with computer facilities, many branches, and a high percentage of intrashifted deposits, there appears to be a large profit potential for preauthorized credit plans. In fact, a combination of an automatic payroll-deposit program and customer-preauthorized payment plans can form a very appealing (and profitable) "market" or "service"

[25] Gary B. Rabn, Vice President, First Wisconsin National Bank of Milwaukee. Presentation before The American Bankers Association's Preauthorized Payments Workshop, New Orleans, Louisiana, January 25–26, 1968.

package, such as the one offered by the Bank of America. An executive vice-president of the country's largest bank described its service as follows: "We are making our computer tape-to-tape program available to our large customers who have computer equipment. They give us a reel of magnetic tape containing the employee's pay and we put it directly into each employee's account with us. Then, we give the employee the service of paying his bills for him by computer, such bills as insurance, rent, mortgage, utilities. If the account runs short, we offer an automatic loan service; and if the account gets too fat, we offer an automatic investment service in a savings account." [26]

For each bill the bank pays, it charges ten cents. On the automatic loans, interest is charged at the rate of 1.5 percent per month. Funds that are shifted automatically into the bank's own savings accounts pay 4 percent yearly.

[26] "Electronic Money," *Forbes*, April 1, 1967, p. 45.

An Electronic
Funds-Transfer
System

Chapter Seven

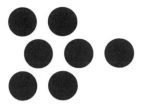

The next step in the evolution of innovation in payment media systems will be the complete elimination of all material forms of money. An electronic funds-transfer system is a computer-controlled accounting system in which all payors and payees have an account in which will be recorded all transfers of credit balances. There will be no need for cash, checks, or credit cards in the future "moneyless society."

This chapter attempts to construct a theoretical framework wherein the logical feasibility for the elimination of what we now use for money can be established. Then follows a description of a hypothetical electronic funds-transfer system as it might logically evolve within the social and institutional framework of our own society.

The historical evolution of payment media systems led to the conclusion in Chapter 2 that the shortcomings of barter constituted the only reason for the eventual use of some single commodity as money. One of the most serious disadvantages of barter, of course, is the lack of a common unit in which to measure the value of goods and services. The use of one standard commodity as money permits the prices of all other goods and services to be expressed in terms of that one commodity.

If the subject of payment media systems were approached from its historical evolution, it would be a natural assumption that the use of some selected commodity as money is the only alternative to a system of barter. Historically, the selection of a single commodity as money *was* the only alternative to barter; theoretically, however, with a standard of value a society could exist without a medium of exchange.

Hypothesize a society such as ours, only with no medium of exchange. Throughout any given day goods are exchanged and services are rendered. Even though no medium of exchange exists, it is not necessary for the goods and services to be bartered.[1] If a man is employed for a standard workday, this will create a *debt* from the employer to the employee. In this case the employer is a buyer of a service and the employee a seller. The employer (a businessman), however, will have

---

[1] See R. G. Hawtrey, *Currency and Credit* (London: Longmans, Green), 1919, Chapter 1.

been and/or will be a seller himself and the employee a buyer. At the end of a given day all buyers and sellers could meet and set off their debts and credits. For the debts and credits to be settled, it is necessary that they be reduced to some common standard of value. The standard of value technically may be called a "money of account" even though there is no medium of exchange.

If at the end of the day everyone could exactly balance his debts against his credits, the next business day could begin with another standard of value. The unit could be completely arbitrary as long as there was a common agreement among all individuals in the market-place. Since, however, it will be virtually impossible for all debts and credits to be perfectly balanced, it will be necessary to continue with the same unit of value for each business day.

Each business day would begin with a record of the previous day's residue of indebtedness. During the process of production, the service rendered by an employee creates a debt from the person (or business firm) to whom the final product belongs. A steel mill might "pay" the wages of its employees by creating a debt to the workmen, but in order for the employees to "spend" their wages the debt must be transferred to someone else. The steel mill can sell only steel. The solution to this problem can be found by the intervention of one who *deals in debts*. The steel mill can assign to the dealer in debts the debts which are owed to it for the sale of its product, and the dealer in debts in return can transfer to himself the steel mill's liabilities to its employees. This process of setting off one debt against another has been described as the use of *credit* as the medium of exchange. If every creditor in society were to assign the debts due him to the dealer in debts, the setting off of all debts in society could cover the entire field of economic activity.

The accepted standard of value simply provides a unit for the measurement of debts. The same unit also provides the measure of value and prices. When goods and services are quoted in terms of prices and a transaction is made, the function of the price merely is to measure the magnitude of the debt incurred by the buyer to the seller.

A dealer in debts and credits is a *banker*. If all debts in society are assigned to the banker, he can set off all liabilities against one another simply by recording all debts and credits on a set of books. If more than one bank exists, each banker would have to set off debts and credits with the other bankers. Of course, another dealer in debts could emerge to which all banks assigned their debts, and it in turn could act as a clearinghouse for the banker. As long as society maintains confidence in the banks, their obligations would supply a perfectly satisfactory means for the discharge of debts, because a debt can be just as adequately canceled against another debt as extinguished by a payment of money. Of course, some of the bank's liabilities could take the form of bank notes, which constitute nothing more than circulating evidences of the bank's debts. The exchange of a bank note, which is defined as money, is another way of transferring a bank debt instead of making the transfer on the books of the bank.[2]

So far in the discussion, the function of the banker has been limited to the settling of debts and credits at the end of the business day. Most individuals in society for various reasons would desire to keep some unexhausted credit to meet future "payments." The reserves of unexhausted credit owned by society amount to undischarged debts (or liabilities) of the bankers. To the extent that these reserves exist at any given time, they equal the bankers' indebtedness to society. Since the bankers are dealers in debt, they do not take liabilities upon themselves without receiving an equal amount of assets.

The steel mill may pay its employees with bank liabilities; however, for the banker to accept such debts he must receive an equal consideration of assets. The banker is in no need of steel, the employer's product; the banker's business is dealing in debts. The banker can accept the liability of the employees' salaries, however, by creating a debt from the employer to the bank. In short, the banker makes a loan rather than acquire the steel mill's product as an offsetting asset. The banker's assets will consist mainly of loans made to producers, who in turn employ the credit in their respective businesses and pay interest to the banker out of the sales revenues they make.

When the banker makes a loan, he creates credit. He assumes an immediate debt to his customer in exchange for the customer's debt to him due at a future time. The banker's obligation (bank credit), either in the form of a bookkeeping entry or in the form of bank notes, meets the customer's needs because it can be assigned away as a means of payment, whereas the customer's own debt may not be readily acceptable either because the payee does not have confidence in the payor's obligation and/or because the payee is not in the business of dealing in debts. The customer's debt to the bank yields interest income to the banker until it is canceled and supplies the banker with an income for providing the service and taking the risks.

The banking system of our present society has come to perform the

[2] Because of the accepted position of the banker as a dealer in debts and the eventual use of these debts as a means of payment, some of the banker's liabilities have come to be defined as "money," i.e., bank notes and demand-deposit liabilities.

function of a giant clearinghouse for the offsetting of debts and credits, and as a great credit machine by making loans and creating debts. In time the general accredibility of bank liabilities by society as a means of offsetting debts has caused the banker's debts to perform the functions of money. The transference of bank debts as a means of payment can be accomplished through a variety of techniques:

1. *Bank notes.* Bank notes simply are pieces of paper which indicate to the holder of the note that the bank is indebted to that holder to the extent of same unit of value. The indebtedness of the bank is transferred when the piece of paper changes hands.

2. *Checks.* A check is a written instrument given by a person, to whom the bank is indebted, to another person ordering the bank to transfer a portion of its indebtedness from the payor to the payee. The bank's debt to the payee may be evidenced by a bookkeeping entry (deposit liability) or by the issuance of bank notes.

3. *Giro Credit Transfer.* A giro credit transfer may be initiated by an oral or written order directly given to the bank requesting that a portion of its indebtedness to the payor be transferred to a named payee.

4. *Bank Credit Card.* A bank credit card can be used to indicate to a payee that the payor has an established credit relationship with the bank. When making a purchase, the payee has the payor sign a sales ticket, which is presented to the bank. The bank creates a debt to the payee and offsets its liability either by canceling an equal debt to the payor or by creating an equal debt from the payor to the bank (making a loan).

5. *Preauthorized Payment.* For debts which are incurred regularly by a payor, the payor may agree to permit the bank to incur indebtedness to a named payee for specific amounts during regular intervals of time through an agreement made in advance with the bank. Again the bank may offset its indebtedness to the payee by canceling an equal debt to the payor or by creating a loan.

All of these techniques have come about because of convenience and institutional arrangements to fulfill one primary function — that of off-setting debts and creating credits by the banking system, the dealer in debts. Until the present, it has been virtually impossible for the banking system to set off and balance its debts and credits at the end of each business day. If, however, all buyers and sellers in the marketplace could inform the banking system of all debts incurred, and to whom, and each bank in the system had the capability of clearing all its debts with all other banks in the system, theoretically there could be a net balancing of debts to cover the whole day's economic activity.

Technical developments in the areas of electronic data-processing, information retrieval systems, and microelectronics have made it technologically feasible for the banking system to set off all of society's debts within a given business day. The next stage in the evolution of payment media systems will be the electronic transference of funds (or setting off of debts and credits) by means of vast on-line, real-time computer systems. A national computer network with regional centers will permit the instantaneous transference of bank debts from payors to payees. Within time most of the existing methods used for the settlement of debts and the exchange of money balances will become totally obsolete.

7.1. The Essential Elements

The basic elements of a future electronic funds-transfer system include (1) a unique personal "identifier," (2) an on-line banking system, and (3) a multitude of on-line retail merchants. Once such a system evolves, it is expected that it will include many other institutional relationships; however, in order to provide a basic understanding of how such a system might work, the discussion here is limited to only the essential components.

7.1.1. The Unique Personal "Identifier." Under an electronic funds-transfer system, each individual will carry an identification card, which will serve as the input to terminal devices connected to a master computer switching system. A series of punched holes in the card will carry the telephone switching number of the individual's bank, the type of account, and his account number.

The account number will play an important part in the computer system; the type of number used will affect other technical parts of the system, such as the storage requirements for accounts within computer memory banks, the time required to locate an account record in the memory, the type of equipment needed to ensure the security of account information, the complexity of the computer programing, and the compatibility of the different components of the system. Thus the establishment of a standard and universal numbering system is one of the first requirements of an electronic funds-transfer system.

One numbering scheme has received particular attention, and it involves the Social Security number. Costs and standardization problems could be reduced greatly by the adoption of a numbering system which already is in widespread use. A major argument in favor of the Social Security number is the fact that most financial institutions must use the number anyway when reporting income from customers' savings accounts, savings shares, trusts, and other income-producing services. In fact, after much study the Personal Identification Project Subcommittee of the American Bankers Association's Committee on Payment Systems has recommended that banks use the Social Security number plus an additional digit for ensuring identification and proper transmission.

Assuming that the Social Security number is adopted as the standard numbering base, there will be the additional need to ensure that the holder of an identification card is in fact the true owner of that card. Several schemes for identification have been proposed; they include a nonerasable signature block, an embedded photograph, a fingerprint, or a voice spectrograph. Of these techniques, the voice spectrograph or "voice print" appears to be the most promising foolproof method for making a positive identification of a cardholder.

A voice spectrograph is the unique pattern which each individual's voice makes on a cathode-ray oscilloscope when pronouncing a word or set of words. By comparing the characteristics of one's voice print with computer-stored records of his sound patterns, the positive identification of an individual can be made. When making a purchase of a relatively high-priced item, the payor could be identified by the statement of a few words into an on-line microphone device or simply a telephone.

7.1.2. The On-Line Banking System. The first and obvious step toward an on-line banking system is for each bank in the system to establish either on- or off-premise computer capabilities. It is expected that most large banks that can afford the investment will establish their own electronic data-processing systems. Small and some medium-sized banks will establish off-premise capabilities either by jointly investing in computer equipment and participating on a time-sharing basis, or by relying on the computer services provided by a correspondent bank.

The nucleus of the on-line banking system will be the regional computer center. Such centers across the nation could be managed and financed much like local clearinghouse operations that are in existence today. The switching computer system at the regional center would link together all banks in its region, and it in turn would link into a national network of regional centers. The national network would not only include the regional centers and the major banks in the system but also the Federal Reserve System and the United States Treasury. Figure 7.1 illustrates the position of the regional computer center and alternate bank configurations.

7.1.3. On-Line Retail Merchants. The key element linking retailers to the regional computer center is a remote terminal device located at the point of sale in the retail establishment. The terminal device must be capable of accepting the customer's identification card and communi-

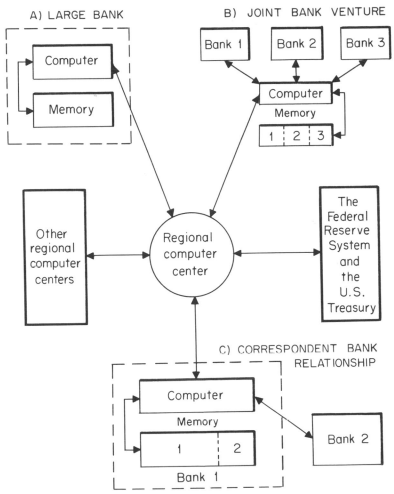

Figure 7.1. Position of the regional computer center and alternate bank configurations.

cating to the customer's bank his account number and the identification number of the retailer's bank and his account number.

The terminal device would be on-line to the regional computer center, which would switch the transmission of data to the cardholder's bank. If the purchase were relatively small, the bank's computer would activate an instantaneous transfer of the amount of the purchase from the payor's demand deposit account to the account of the payee. A green light or some other signal on the retailer's terminal would indicate that the transaction was consummated.

If the purchase price were relatively high, the bank's computer would signal the retailer by means of a yellow light that positive identification of the cardholder would be necessary. The customer would then speak one or two words into the device's microphone. The spoken words would be transmitted to the regional center, where the cardholder's voice print would be compared to the spectrograph on file. If the terminal indicates by means of a red light that the cardholder is not the rightful owner, the merchant could seize the card and notify the local authorities. If, however, the proper identification verification is made, the bank can make the demand-deposit transfer, provided that the payor's account balance is sufficient. When an account balance is insufficient, the bank may cancel the sale or credit the retailer's account and create a loan to the customer.

When a customer has a preestablished line of credit, a purchase can be made by a simple bookkeeping adjustment. But if the purchase price were to exceed the line of credit, a special loan would need to be made. In such a case the bank's computer would draw on the regional center's credit-information file, which provides the data necessary to evaluate the customer's credit worthiness. If the loan is made, the merchant's account is immediately credited and the green light indicates that the transaction has been completed. The on-line connections of the credit-information and personal-identification files are illustrated in Figure 7.2.

The credit-information file contains historical credit information on each individual living within the area of the regional computer center. Such data may be supplied and maintained by the participating banks; or the files may be maintained by the credit bureau industry, which would have to acquire the necessary electronic data-processing equipment and be on an on-line relationship with the regional computer centers.

7.2. The National Network

In order for interregional transfers of funds to be made, there must be an integrated, national network of computer systems. It is expected that multiregional communications will be possible through at least three types of networks: (1) on-line communications between regional computer centers, (2) direct lines of communication between private financial institutions, and (3) the computerized wire transfer service of the Federal Reserve System.

7.2.1. Transfers between Regional Computer Centers. Transfers of funds among regional comptuer centers will be made over lines directly connecting each regional center with all other centers in the national network. From the standpoint of the payor, an interregional electronic-

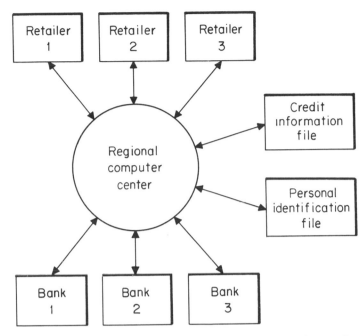

Figure 7.2. On-line connections of the credit-information and personal-identification files.

funds transfer will be made much like an intraregional transfer. The payee's regional number, bank number, and bank account number will be dialed into a terminal device by the payor. The payee's regional number will establish through the regional switching computer centers an immediate communications link between the payor's bank and the payee's bank.

Figure 7.3 illustrates an interregional electronic-funds transfer. (1) The payor establishes a communications link through a terminal to his regional computer center; (2) the switching computer connects the payor with his bank; (3A) when the payee's regional number is dialed; (4) the bank's computer, through its regional center, is connected to the payee's regional center; (5) the dialed payee's bank number and bank account number permit the payor bank to credit the proper account at the payee bank; and (6) the payor is notified that the funds have been transferred.

7.2.2. Transfers among Private Financial Institutions. Because of the large volume of transactions among some large financial institutions, they will find it convenient and more economical to lease an interconnecting open line of communications. Most banks and other institutions making interregional transfers, however, will find it more economical to share open lines from one region to another via the system of regional computer centers.

An interregional transfer of funds involving two banks with a direct open line of communications is illustrated in Figure 7.3. The direct funds transfer eliminates steps (4) and (5). The computer system of the payor bank links directly to the payee bank, and the transference of funds bypasses the network of regional computer centers (3B).

7.2.3. Transfers through the Federal Reserve System. The Federal Reserve banks and branches will make electronic funds transfers through their own computer and wire facilities. This system was discussed in Chapter 4, and was to begin operation in November 1969.

Because a nationwide electronic funds-transfer system will be implemented gradually, for some time there will continue to be a need for much interdistrict settlement of bank balances due to the check clearing process. The computer network linking the Board of Governors of the Federal Reserve System, the Treasury Department, and the thirty-

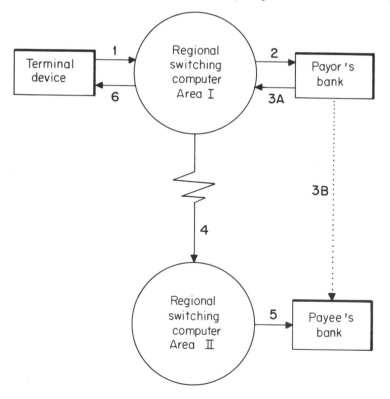

Figure 7.3. An interregional electronic funds transfer.

six Federal Reserve banks and branches will be the primary network through which the large volume of federal government transfers is made. In addition to funds transfers, this system will supply a vast amount of district and regional economic information to the fiscal and monetary authorities for use in implementing economic stabilization policies.

7.3. Other Participants in the Electronic Funds-Transfer System

7.3.1. Business Firms. The advantages of an electronic funds-transfer system to individuals, retailers, and banks will also apply to other business firms. Payrolls, for example, could be made by simply transferring funds from the employer's bank account through the regional computer center to all of the employees' banks and proper accounts. For large firms with computer facilities, the entire company's payroll could be handled in a matter of minutes, eliminating much employee time and expensive paperwork.

With funds being transferred instantaneously, there would be no need for a business firm to carry large amounts of receivables and payables. Corporate financial managers would become increasingly concerned over the time value of money. They would be able to plan and manage their working capital needs in such ways as to synchronize the inflows and outflows of money balances, thus keeping short-term accounts to a minimum.

7.3.2. Home Users. Every telephone, whether in a home, hotel room, office, or even a pay booth, is a potential remote terminal device for electronic-funds transfer. An American Telephone and Telegraph Company specially designed touch-tone telephone is in use at the present time in a pilot electronic funds-transfer system.[3] The basic telephone unit of the touch-tone phone is the same as existing units; all that is needed is the American Telephone and Telegraph's "card-dialer," which is capable of reading hole-punched cards.

The home unit would accept an individual's "money card," and permit funds to be transferred from the payor's account to any other account. The necessary data would be inserted into the touch-tone phone, and an audioresponse generated from the payor's bank would verify orally the numbers punched into the phone. The touch-tone phone will permit most retail banking to be conducted electronically from the customer's own home.

[3] The pilot system is managed with the cooperation of American Telephone and Telegraph, the Bank of Delaware, and International Business Machines. The bank's "electronic credit card" enables the cardholder to purchase merchandise from a local merchant in Wilmington by inserting his card in the retailer's touch-tone phone. The salesman dials the bank and punches out the details of the sale. Funds are transferred from the customer's account to that of the merchant, and the sale is consummated.

7.3.3. Nonbank Financial Institutions. Depending upon the actual course of development toward a future electronic funds-transfer system, there is a host of financial intermediaries other than banks which will need to find a place in the cashless-checkless society. Some of these institutions will find it increasingly difficult to compete in many markets with commercial banks. Others, however, will continue to serve markets that banks have not entered, and some undoubtedly will serve new markets as they develop.

Institutions such as insurance companies, savings and loans associations, and other credit grantors eventually may occupy on-line positions to the regional computer centers. If a customer cannot find satisfactory loan or other service accommodation at his bank, he may simply dial another institution. These intermediaries, with the banks, could share the use and operational costs of the regional computer centers, thus enabling the high fixed costs of the computer equipment to be spread over a large volume of transactions.

The Implications of   Chapter Eight
a Future Electronic
Funds-Transfer
System for
Commercial Banking
and Other Industries

Because a future electronic funds-transfer system will evolve rather than emerge suddenly as a major innovation in the payment process, the operation of such a system could be undertaken in a variety of forms by any number of types or combinations of institutions. The range and character of alternative possibilities create an untold number of potential implications for commercial banking and other industries heavily committed to various forms of credit transactions.

The basic technologies for electronic funds transfer essentially are in existence already in the form of third-generation computer systems incorporating advanced time-sharing techniques and real-time communications capabilities, increased mass-information storage capacity and increased processing speeds, and improved terminal devices that permit unlimited direct systems access by large numbers of users for a variety of information-processing services. The software needed to implement a future electronic funds-transfer system should soon be available, including systems design and consideration of problems not yet resolved. The future implementation of such a system seems assured because of its inherent economies and convenience and because of the increasing pressure to find means of coping with the growing volume of paper surrounding the present debt-settlement process.

Determinants of the eventual structure of the electronic funds-transfer system include economic feasibility, in terms of the cost advantages of new technologies compared with present methods of payment settlement and credit extension; legal constraints imposed by regulatory authorities; and psychological and sociological constraints imposed by possible resistance to such a system by the consumer.

The most likely changes in the present payments system will be those which involve the introduction of a minimum of institutional changes. In short, innovation evolves via the paths of least resistance and most recognizable benefits. The commercial banking industry, with its well-developed payment and credit systems, appears to be best suited to securing the preeminent position in the future electronic funds-transfer system.

The dominant position of the commercial banks, however, is *not* assured. There will be many other industries which may compete with commercial banks in their attempt to establish positions in tomorrow's "cashless-checkless" society. In all likelihood the industry which seizes the initiative will exert the primary influence on the determination of the structure of a future electronic funds-transfer system. The evidence would indicate that progressive bankers are taking the initiative, and it has been assumed that the commercial banking industry will continue to be the primary force affecting the payments process. Accordingly, the analysis of implications in this and the following chapter will be made under this assumption. It will not be assumed, however, that other affected industries will stand by idly; it will be necessary to analyze the reactions and implications for these other industries.

This chapter will present an analysis of the probable changes in the structure and functioning of the commercial-banking industry as occasioned by the progressive stages of automation in the payments mechanism. Then it will focus attention on the implications for other industries, including savings banks and savings and loan associations, insurance companies, personal and commercial finance companies, credit bureaus and personal credit information services, credit-card companies, and retailers.

8.1. The Commercial-Banking Industry

8.1.1. Increased Automation and Changing Personnel Needs. It was stressed in Chapter 7 that the first step toward an on-line banking system would be for each bank to establish either on- or off-premise computer capabilities. Many banks already have introduced computer automation to meet the growing demands of check processing. The continued growth in the volume of checks and the successful application of computer capabilities to other banking operations and services have enticed more banks to establish computer capabilities. Computer services have been obtained by banks through the purchase of computers or through the use of computers of correspondent banks, bank cooperatives, service bureaus, or joint ventures.

The results of an American Bankers Association survey in the mid-1960s indicate that banks for the most part have computerized or are in the process of computerizing their check-processing operations. Another survey completed in late 1965 by the National Association of Bank Auditors and Controllers demonstrated the trend in recent years for banks, particularly the larger ones, toward automation. Table 8.1 summarizes the results of the survey. By mid-1967, a spokesman for the American Bankers Association estimated that three thousand banks had established computer capabilities and that some 1,358 other banks

Table 8.1.   **Banks with Computer Capabilities (by resource class).**

Resource Class (millions of dollars)	No. of Banks in United States	No. of Banks Reporting	No. of Banks with On-Premise Computers	No. of Banks with Off-Premise Computers	Total Banks Reporting Use of Computers	
					No.	Percentage
$100 and over	368	248	237	2	239	97
$50–$100	313	119	60	18	78	65
$25–$50	617	192	37	50	87	45
$10–$25	2,125	244	4	58	62	25
Under $10	10,253	267	—	56	56	21
Total	13,676	1,070	338	184	522	

Source: *1965–1966 Directory of Bank Automation.*

were at the stage of actively planning for an automation system.[1] Estimates have been made to indicate that by 1970, the banks which conduct over 90 percent of the dollar volume of banking operations in this country will own computers or have arrangements for computer operations off premises.[2]

Over the next decade there will be a substantial shift in the personnel needs of banks that are automating. Experience has indicated that once having acquired computers to automate its demand-deposit and check-processing operations, a bank has automated its other operations, including savings accounts; proof and transit; consumer, mortgage, and commercial loans; and personal and corporate trust operations. There will be an increasing demand for programers and computer technicians, who are already in short supply.

8.1.2. Reduced Costs in Check Processing. As demand-deposit transfers become increasingly automated, there will be less and less check sorting and re-sorting and check shipment from bank to bank or from bank to customer. Storage requirements for checks will be progressively reduced, and there will be less and less kited checks, check float, and manual processing of checks.[3] Once the necessary electronic data-processing equipment has been acquired and a satisfactory volume of transactions

[1] "Stepping Stones to the Checkless Society," *Burroughs Clearing House*, June 1967, p. 23.
[2] See Allan H. Anderson and others, *An Electronic Cash and Credit System* (New York: American Management Association, 1966), Chapter 4.
[3] See George W. Mitchell, "Effects of Automation on the Structure and Functioning of Banking," *American Economic Review*, May 1966, pp. 159–166.

is automated, there should be a considerable cost savings to the banks. A spokesman for the Federal Reserve Bank of New York has stated:

Preliminary indications are that if a DFT [Direct Funds Transfer] system is in widespread operation by 1975 — which is fully predicted as a likely date — the average cost per transaction will be 7½ cents, with a spread of from 3 cents to 12 cents in individual transactions. Present costs of the demand deposit or checking account system appear to run to about 13 cents per transaction, to which must be added another 12 cents per transaction if the transaction involves an extension of credit. If these figures are even nearly right . . . use of the DFT system in 1975 could at best save 17½ cents per transaction on average and at worst save 5½ cents per transaction on average.[4]

8.1.3. Expanded Services and New Sources of Revenue. Instead of charging for checks or imposing a monthly service charge, electronic funds transfer will enable banks to levy a charge for each transaction made by their customers. Such charges will be deducted automatically from customers' accounts and will appear on the customers' monthly statements. Present charges made by banks for preauthorized payments average about ten cents per transaction.

With an electronic funds-transfer system it would seem logical and practical for the banking industry to increase its activities substantially beyond the accounting for debt settlement. A commercial bank will be in a position to handle much of a customer's accounting both antecedent and subsequent to funds transfers. For a commercial customer, a bank's services could extend logically to include much of the firm's accounting and working capital management. By virtue of its central position in the payments process, the bank would be able to perform the accounting and financing of receivables, billing and collecting operations, cash flow management, and financial planning.[5]

Banks will expand into many new areas, providing financial advice to individuals as well as businesses. Many services will be integrated and marketed as "service packages." Banks have already begun to extend their customer services and tie them together. For example, the First National City Bank of New York has begun operating a travel agency. When individuals buy tickets, they are offered travelers' checks. They also may apply for membership in Carte Blanches (at the time a Citibank subsidiary), and they may arrange to finance their tickets and travel expenses. Speaking of this new customer service, one of the bank's executives said, "We get them coming and going." [6]

[4] "Hard Figures and Considered Judgments on Progress Towards Checkless Society," *American Banker,* February 17, 1967.
[5] D. W. Richardson, *Payment Media Systems Innovation: The Prospects for the Banking Industry* (Austin: The College of Business Administration, The University of Texas at Austin, July 1967), Research Paper 67–16.
[6] "Electronic Money," *Forbes,* April 1, 1967, p. 43.

8.1.4. Greater Emphasis on Time and Savings Deposits. With better management of customers' cash flows coupled with a bank's ability to transfer automatically excess demand deposit balances into interest-earning savings accounts and other investment outlets, it would be expected that the average-size demand-deposit balance would become smaller. Also with preauthorized lines of credit available, the individual customer would have less need of large deposit balances. Lower demand-deposit balances will reduce a major source of "interest-free" funds for banks; however, revenues from additional service charges should more than make up for decreases in demand-deposit balances, much of which will be shifted into the bank's own savings accounts. Such a phenomenon will not occur overnight. During the last decade bankers have become increasingly aware of a trend toward greater time and savings deposits, which recently culminated for the first time in years in a greater level of aggregate time and savings deposits than demand deposits.

8.1.5. New Forms of Competition. Due to advantages in raising long-term funds and other economies of scale, it is much easier for large banks to acquire computer equipment and implement electronic funds-transfer services. For small banks to compete they will have to strengthen their correspondent relationships and engage in cooperative ventures with other small banks. According to George Mitchell of the Board of Governors of the Federal Reserve System, "We now have a system of 14,000 banks, but some 2,000 of them are doing 90% of the work. In the electronic system, you can look for a decrease in the number of banks. It's going to be quite difficult for a small bank to compete." [7]

It would appear that progression toward an electronic funds-transfer system certainly will put added pressures for increased concentration in the banking structure. Of course, the actual decline of the number of banks will depend in large measure upon changes in state branch banking laws. In those states with no branching or highly restrictive branching, there will be increased pressure and tendencies toward chain and group banking.

Electronic funds transfer, automation, and closed-circuit television technology will enable the large banks to implement vast systems of remote tellers. Remote tellers could be located in shopping centers, post offices, and other convenient areas, thus reducing the necessity for bank customers to visit the bank in person. Equipment manufacturers envision a remote teller as consisting of a combination vending machine and television screen. The customer and the teller in the bank's downtown headquarters will be able to see each other and carry on a

[7] *Ibid.*

conversation. The customer will be able to make deposits and with-drawals, obtain loans, and transact other business with the machine, which is controlled by the teller. Remote tellers will enable a bank to compete in almost any market area and provide most of the services extended by the bank's main offices.

Progression toward an electronic funds-transfer system will demonstrate the greater competitive positions of banks which already are heavily committed to bank credit cards and preauthorized payments. Not only will these banks have much of the necessary equipment and valuable experience, they will have developed the necessary relationships with both merchants and cardholders. At the present time it is envisioned that the major obstacle to a fully implemented electronic funds-transfer system is the individual.[8] The banking community will have to engage in a large campaign aimed toward educating the customer and selling the consumer on the advantages of a new means of payment. To the individual, an innovation that requires the least amount of change in his habits will be most readily accepted. For those consumers who are already used to using bank credit cards and preauthorized payments, there will be a much easier transition to their position in an electronic funds-transfer system.

8.2. Savings Banks and Savings and Loan Associations

8.2.1. Savings Banks.
Mutual savings banks accept savings deposits and make loans primarily in the urban residential mortgage market. Savings banks are chartered under state laws in eighteen states located primarily in the northeast (New York, Massachusetts, and Pennsylvania are the major savings-bank states). The extent of services offered by savings banks is limited by state regulations; services now permissible in all or some of the savings-bank states include: (1) regular and school savings accounts; (2) special higher-yielding savings accounts, such as bonus accounts; (3) savings-bank life insurance; (4) unsecured personal loans; (5) mortgage loans; and (6) demand-deposit accounts. As the result of a recent court decision, savings banks in New Jersey now also have the right to offer demand-deposit accounts.

Although the size of the mutual savings bank industry is relatively small, its characteristics make it a potential competitor to the commercial banking system in the area of electronic funds transfer. In several of the states, savings banks have already implemented a pre-authorized-payment service. At the present time savings banks come closer than any other financial institution to offering the services of

[8] See William D. Smith, "The Checkless Society: Human Beings Causing the Chief Delays," *The New York Times,* May 21, 1967, Section 3, p. 8; and A. K. Cary, "Our Moneyless Society," *Burroughs Clearing House,* March 1960, p. 43.

commercial banks, and the industry is in the process of expanding its services. The 1966 annual report of the National Association of Mutual Savings Banks indicates the industry's awareness of its opportunity to become the individual's and family's major financial service center. In essence the report states that

(1) the development of a safe, efficient and convenient facility through which individuals may transfer funds and make payments is necessary if savings banks are to serve their customers' financial needs effectively; and (2) the association has undertaken a study of the basic policy considerations involved in establishing a transfer service for savings bank depositors.[9]

A significant development which places greater emphasis on the future role of the savings-bank industry is the Federal Charter bill currently before Congress.[10] If passed, the act would permit the federal chartering of mutual savings banks in any state, and the banks would be supervised by the Federal Home Loan Bank. In a relatively short time, such a law would permit a nationwide network of savings banks which would compete with commercial banks. If federal chartering of savings banks were permitted, it is expected that the regulations and supervisory agencies affecting this new type of institution would be much more reasonable and lenient than many of the outdated regulations affecting the commercial banking industry. The institution of modern regulations and laws governing federally chartered savings banks would surely give them a competitive advantage over commercial banks.

8.2.2. Savings and Loan Associations. Savings and loan associations accept savings and make loans primarily in the residential mortgage market. They may be incorporated under either state or national law. Those incorporated under national law must be mutual associations, while state-chartered institutions may be either mutual or stock companies; the mutual type is dominant in nearly all states. All associations, both federal and state institutions, that are insured by the Federal Savings and Loan Insurance Corporation come under the supervision of the Federal Home Loan Bank.

Although the savings and loan industry is much larger than the savings-bank industry, it does not offer as great a potential competitive force to the commercial banks. At the present time there are considerable restrictions placed on the lending powers of savings and loan associations. In fact, the progression toward an electronic funds-transfer system could hurt severely the savings and loan industry.

[9] Richard S. Mathews, "The Role of Other Industries in a Checkless Society" (unpublished manuscript).
[10] Much attention has concentrated recently on the provisions of H.R. 13718 currently before the Congress.

Forbes reported that "Many savings and loan officers, accepting the advent of electronic banking, believe the savings and loans will have to merge with or imitate the commercial banks or disappear." [11]

The passage of the Federal Charter bill proposed by the savings banks could have important implications for the savings and loan industry. The competitive position of the savings and loan institutions vis-à-vis the commercial banks could be improved immensely by their being rechartered as federal savings banks. The movement toward an electronic funds-transfer system and the possible passage of a Federal Charter bill would provide substantial motivation for the integration of the savings-bank and savings and loan industries into a national system of federally chartered savings banks. Such a system could offer a broad scope of financial services and compete aggressively with the commercial banking industry for the predominant position in a future electronic funds-transfer system.

8.3. Insurance Companies

The primary function of the insurance industry is the spreading of economic risks, but in the process insurance companies amass great amounts of funds which place them in the extremely important position of holding the largest pool of savings among the private nonmonetary financial intermediaries. Life-insurance companies alone have combined assets of over $175 billion, or approximately one-fifth of the assets of all financial institutions.

Life-insurance companies operate under state charters, and they are regulated by state insurance commissions. Generally, state laws restrict life-insurance companies' investments to debt obligations — high-grade bonds and real-estate mortgages. Some state laws permit the purchase of a limited amount of corporate stock and the placement of a part of their funds in certain types of commercial and industrial properties. Private insurance companies represent the largest source of external capital used by American industry. In addition to investments in corporate bonds, notes, and stock, insurance companies extend credit in return for mortgage notes on business property. This represents the chief source of intermediate and working capital for small business firms, especially those that are not incorporated.

Although there appears to be no organized effort by the insurance companies at the present time, some insurance executives envision their industry as occupying a key position in a future electronic funds-transfer system. The president of one large insurance firm made the following remarks in a recent speech:

Our [the insurance industry's] computer skills and the possible ex-

[11] "Electronic Money," *Forbes,* p. 43.

tension of them defy the imagination. Who is to say that one day we might not handle all of a man's salary, allotting it to reflect his individual desires in the world of electronic money? Might we not implement his total personal financial planning, using much the same methods now used in estate planning programs? Why should banks monopolize the credit card system of paying bills? [12]

8.4. Personal and Commercial Finance Companies

8.4.1. Personal-Finance Companies.

Personal-finance companies (small-loan companies) operate under the provisions of the Uniform Small Loan Law adopted by most of the states. These companies are exempt from usury laws applicable to other lenders, and the interest rates they charge and the maximum amounts they may lend are fixed by law. Small-loan companies make loans based on chattel mortgages, wage assignment, and in some cases on unsecured notes provided that the borrower is a good credit risk. These types of loans are generally referred to as "high-cost, high-risk" loans.

Personal-finance companies came into existence because federal and state governments did not permit commercial banks to adjust their interest rates so as to compensate them for the greater risks and higher costs involved in extending certain types of credit. As a result, commercial banks have not actively sought business in the small-loan market. In fact, most banks fail to make a profit on any personal loans of less than $350.

With the advent of the bank credit card, however, issuing banks have discovered a technique through which many small loans can be profitable. Those commercial banks with a cash-advance feature on their credit cards are currently acquiring some of the more stable finance-company customers. For the small-loan customer, it is considerably more convenient (and less embarrassing) to present his bank credit card and obtain a "cash advance" with no questions asked than it is for him to visit a small-loan office and fill out a loan application and other forms and possibly be rejected.

When a fully implemented electronic funds-transfer system becomes a reality, nearly all consumers will have ready access to small loans via their bank money-cards. In addition, preauthorized lines of credit extended by commercial banks will become *de facto* overdraft privileges, which will lessen the necessity for customers to seek small-loan accommodation elsewhere. These innovations by the commercial banks will make it increasingly difficult for small-loan companies to survive the progression toward an electronic funds-transfer system.

8.4.2. Commercial-Finance Companies.

A commercial-finance company

[12] "Stepping Stones to the Checkless Society," *Burroughs Clearing House,* p. 77.

specializes in accounts-receivable financing or the outright purchase of a firm's accounts receivable (factoring). The procedure of accounts-receivable financing has been described in the following way:

The business firm passes its own credits, makes shipments on its usual terms, and handles its own collections. As it makes shipments, it sends copies of the invoices it wishes to finance, with evidence of shipment or delivery, to the financing institution. The latter immediately sends its check to the firm for the amount of the agreed-upon advance. As the firm receives checks from debtors in payment of invoices financed, it endorses them "Pay to any Bank or Bankers," and forwards them to the financing institution. By arrangement with its banks, this institution deposits the checks without its name appearing as an endorser — so that the debtors are not made aware that it has handled the checks or has made advances against the receivables of the firms. The funds advanced against these receivables are thus automatically repaid as the firm's customers pay the invoices financed. Hence, there are no maturities to meet. Moreover, each day as checks of trade debtors are received by the financing institution from the firm being financed, this institution sends its check to the firm, remitting the difference between the amounts advanced and the amounts the firm's customers have paid on the invoices advanced.[13]

In essence, the bank credit card is simply a means for a commercial bank to finance a firm's accounts receivable. In a "cashless-checkless" society centered around the commercial banking system, accounts receivable would be transferred immediately into "cash" (instantaneous deposit credit), and thus the working capital needs of business firms would be supplied by the banks. Bank money cards will compete directly with the services currently offered by commercial-finance companies.

In several areas of the country, competition between commercial-bank credit cards has forced the merchant discount down to as low as 2 percent. As competition increases, it is expected that discounts will reach minimum levels across the country. The banks with large numbers of cardholders and participating business firms will receive sufficient income from the extension of consumer credit to permit low returns from merchants. The credit extended by commercial-finance companies and factoring companies is relatively costly, making it much more desirable to finance receivables through the use of bank credit cards or (eventually) money cards.

In addition to the credit cost advantages of financing receivables through commercial banks, there would be other benefits. First, the

[13] Clyde W. Phelps, *Accounts Receivable Financing As a Method of Business Finance*, Studies in Commercial Financing, No. 2, Commercial Credit Company (1957), p. 17. Also see Clyde W. Phelps, *The Role of Factoring in Modern Business Finance*, Studies in Commercial Finance No. 1, Commercial Credit Company (1956).

bank assumes all responsibilities for collection and bad-debt losses; whereas commercial-finance companies often make loans on receivables on a "with-recourse" basis. Second, there has existed for some time the attitude that the payment of debts to a finance company or factor is a signal of financial weakness, a final step short of liquidation. Therefore, in many cases of accounts-receivable. financing, secrecy is considered a vital element (as described in the quotation presented earlier in this chapter). Even though there has been a gradual breakdown in this attitude, it still persists to a large extent. No such feeling, however, has developed with respect to commercial banks, and customers freely make credit-card payments to their banks with no thought that the firms with which they do business are in any financial difficulty. One would expect that the same favorable attitude would continue to exist whether the customer were an individual bank cardholder or another business firm.

In short, progression toward an electronic funds-transfer system will pose serious threats to the commercial finance industry. In the "cashless-checkless" society, commercial banks will become the central source for all bookkeeping transactions. It will be a logical extension from this pivotal position for banks to provide a host of financial services for their commercial customers that heretofore have been provided by other institutions. One California bank executive says that "automatic fund transfer will begin to work much faster for corporations than it will for individuals." He expects that commercial banks eventually will manage all of a firm's working capital, "almost to the point of producing the company's trial balance." [14]

8.5. Credit Bureaus and Personal Credit-Information Services

At the present time credit bureaus and personal credit-information services are not competitive with commercial banks. They provide a much needed service to the banks as well as retailers and other credit grantors. The credit-information industry supplies historical data on individuals which are used by lenders to evaluate a customer's credit risk. The availability of such information will become increasingly important to the commercial banking system as it becomes more heavily committed in the consumer finance market.

For several years into the future, credit-information suppliers will play a vital role in advancing the "cashless-checkless" society. Beyond several years, however, the position of this industry will depend to a large extent on the degree of initiative it takes in securing its survival. Currently there is sufficient evidence to indicate that the banking community is not entirely satisfied with the services now provided by the

[14] "Electronic Money," *Forbes,* p. 45.

credit-information industry. A spokesman for the American Bankers Association has written recently, "For at least two years, I have advocated the development in this country of a consumer-oriented credit bureau industry, which would do for consumer credit what Dun and Bradstreet does for the business sector." [15] Looking into the future a bank president has stated,

If we [bankers] are to become guardians of the financial affairs of our respective communities, better methods for correction and control must be considered. The suppliers of money will have to reconsider present methods of arriving at credit worthiness in a growing, complex population. The amount of data necessary to provide adequate information concerning any one consumer or borrower will become more and more difficult to compile and handle. . . . The weak link in the total system of credit information . . . is the lack of sufficient current reports at local or national credit bureaus.[16]

Those commercial banks that already have obtained electronic data-processing equipment and offer credit cards have built up a considerable amount of financial data on consumers. Progression toward an electronic funds-transfer system indicates that banks will need direct access to the financial records of all consumers and businesses. If these data are not supplied by the credit-information industry, banks will need to continue compiling the information themselves. If the commercial-banking industry collects sufficient financial data, there will be little need for an autonomous credit-information service.

It should be pointed out that even if the credit-information industry takes the initiative to automate its credit files (which many large credit bureaus have done or are now doing) and improve the quality of its information, it may be more convenient and economical for banks to store their own information anyway. To be participants in a future electronic funds-transfer system, it will be necessary for each bank to have computer capabilities and be on an on-line relationship with other banks and its respective regional computer center. Since the banks will have the necessary equipment and have ready access to financial information by virtue of their automatic payment relationship with individuals and business firms, it would be reasonable to expect that the banking system will be in the most favorable position to supply credit information not only to itself but to its customers as well. Should the commercial banking industry be limited, however, by regulatory actions or legal restrictions from operating such a system, there will be a great need for a separate credit-information industry.

[15] Dale L. Reistad, "The Coming Cashless Society," *Business Horizons,* Fall 1967.
[16] William H. Westrup, "Needed: A Central Source for Consumer Credit Data," *Burroughs Clearing House,* December 1966, pp. 67–68.

8.6. Credit-Card Companies

At the present time there is not a great deal of market overlapping between bank credit cards and the three major travel and entertainment credit cards. Over the next several years, however, it is expected that commercial banks will move more and more into the travel and entertainment credit market. Currently many banks are expanding the use of their credit cards by signing up motels, hotels, and transportation firms. A few banks have launched two credit card programs, one card to be used primarily for retail purchases and the other, for higher-income customers, to be used for travel and entertainment.

For several reasons commercial banks have inherent advantages over nonbank institutions offering credit cards. As was stressed earlier, commercial banks are in the central position in the payments mechanism, which makes the bank card a logical extension of their existing services. By virtue of this position the commercial bank can provide innumerable ancillary services that nonbank institutions cannot. Consequently, as the commercial banking system progresses toward an electronic funds-transfer system (substituting "money cards" for bank credit cards), existing credit-card companies will be forced to merge with commercial banks or other financial institutions in order to survive.

Credit-card companies do have the advantage of experience and a large number of existing customers. As commercial banks have accelerated their entry into the credit-card field, they have found it advantageous to obtain controlling interests in nonbank credit-card companies, as in the case of the Maryland National Bank and Charg-It of Baltimore. Mergers of the large travel and entertainment credit-cards companies have already begun. As indicated earlier, the controlling interest in Carte Blanche is now owned by the Avco Corporation, and Diners' Club has a service company which manages nearly fifty bank credit-card systems.

8.7. Retailers

Retailers are one of the three basic elements in a future electronic funds-transfer system. The retail merchant, placed on-line to the regional computer center, will provide the crucial link between the customer and his bank when consummating a transaction. Because of this key position of the retailer, it will be helpful to divide the analysis of implications for retailers into two sections. The first section will describe the implications for retailers during the progression toward an electronic funds-transfer system. These implications will be extremely important in the determination of the rapidity and the extent to which the "cashless-checkless" society evolves over the next decade. It will be vital for the commercial banking system to win the acceptance and cooperation of the retail merchant and to convince him of the advantages of electronic funds transfer. The second section, under the assumption of a bank-centered "cashless-checkless" society, will describe the implications for retailers of a fully implemented system.

8.7.1. Progression Toward an Electronic Funds-Transfer System. The first step, from the retailer's point of view, toward an electronic funds-transfer system is the acceptance and promotion of the bank credit card. Many small- and medium-size retailers currently are taking this step, as indicated in Chapter 6. In fact, the first bank credit-card program was in large part initiated by retailers. According to Arthur T. Roth, Chairman and Chief Executive of the Franklin National Bank, his bank's credit-card program was prompted by local retail merchants. In 1951 the bank had just merged with the South Shore Trust Company in Rockville Centre, a town on the south shore of Long Island. Mr. Roth was invited to attend a Chamber of Commerce meeting and to explain the improvements which the bank planned to make in its services. In the midst of the discussion a local merchant was quoted as saying, "That's all very fine, but if you want to provide a real service for the retailers in town, develop some way for us to compete with the surburban branches of the New York City department stores with their charge accounts. We can compete with them on price and quality but we can't afford to carry charge accounts." [17]

According to Mr. Roth, "the use and purpose of our Franklin card was designed to help the small merchant." Apparently the local merchants derived significant benefits from the Franklin credit card. Roth stated, "Many small merchants were able to increase their volume because of charge account service. Also, many were saved from going out of business." [18]

The dynamic changes in retailing since World War II have accented the need for expanding customer services. One of the major services demanded by retail customers in recent years is the granting of retail credit. Competitive pressures have forced most retailers to offer credit to their customers, and consumers have come to view the extension of retail credit as an expected convenience. Because of these developments the small- or medium-size merchant often finds himself in a financial squeeze. The merchant's customers demand expensive credit

---

[17] Arthur T. Roth, Chairman and Chief Executive, Franklin National Bank of New York. Presentation before the National Credit-Card Conference of The American Bankers Association, Chicago, Illinois, November 9, 1967.
[18] *Ibid.*

and his suppliers want quick payments. Thus, the more he sells, the more difficult it becomes to supply his working-capital needs. A situation like this appears to be ready made for the bank credit card.

A study of charge-account banking in the Sixth Federal Reserve District indicated which merchants were most likely to benefit from bank charge plans. They are (1) merchants whose standard markups are large enough not to make credit selling prohibitive; (2) merchants whose merchandise prices are small enough that customers can pay within the time limits set by the banks;[19] (3) merchants who are small and ordinarily find that the operation of their own credit department would be too difficult and expensive; and (4) merchants who sell goods rather than services.[20,21]

When selling merchants on charge-account banking, bank representatives indicate that their service will help the retailer to expand sales; improve his competitive position; increase customer goodwill; permit immediate conversion of receivables into "cash"; reduce credit problems, bad-debt losses, and costs; and allow him to devote more time to merchandising and selling. The actual experience of retailers was reported in a survey of 489 merchants in the Sixth Federal Reserve District. Table 8.2 indicates the results of the survey, which concentrated on the year 1963.

Generally, the experience of merchants in the Sixth District with charge-account banking was favorable. The greatest objection by retailers was that the costs were too high; merchant discounts averaged 5 to 6 percent. Since that time, however, discounts have been reduced considerably, largely removing this objection. Even though merchant discounts in many areas of the country are down to 2 and 3 percent, competition among bank card plans has added new inconveniences for the merchant.

In areas with several competing bank credit cards, merchants feel obligated to participate as members in each bank's plan. Bank credit-

[19] This criterion for the most part is no longer applicable since most bank credit-card programs now permit cardholders to extend their balances over several months' time.
[20] Annette Pike Woodley and H. Ellsworth Steele, "Charge Account Banking in the Sixth Federal Reserve District," *Atlanta Economic Review,* November 1966, pp. 4–5.
[21] The types of businesses which found bank charge-account plans most beneficial included children's and women's ready-to-wear stores, drug stores, fuel oil dealers, garages and automotive parts dealers, general merchandise stores, jewelry and gift shops, and sporting-goods stores. The service industries which found membership in bank charge plans satisfactory included beauty shops, insurance agencies, laundry and dry cleaning establishments, pest control establishments, and professional workers such as dentists, opticians, and veterinarians.

Table 8.2. Effects of Charge-Account Banking Experienced by Merchants in the Sixth Federal Reserve District, 1963.

Effect	All Merchants (489)	Merchants Who Previously Offered Credit (381)	Merchants Who Did Not Previously Offer Credit (108)
Sales have increased since joining	54%	53%	57%
Impulse sales have increased	32	29	44
Sales of higher-quality merchandise have been promoted	31	29	39
Store traffic has increased	33	30	43
Customer goodwill has improved	33	31	40
Suggestive selling has been easier	49	46	59
Competitive position has improved	47	44	54
More time has been made available for merchandising	19	19	20

Source: *Atlanta Economic Review*, November 1966.

cardholders expect merchants to honor whatever bank card they may present. Most banks require their member merchants to maintain an account in their bank, and this necessitates the retailer's having un-needed account balances and the inconvenience of banking at several institutions. Besides account splitting, retailers experience problems with incompatible imprinters and sales-slip sorting. At the same time, many retailers find that they cannot completely eliminate their own credit functions, since many customers have not acquired bank credit cards but still demand account credit.[22]

At the present time it would appear that bank credit-card programs have helped the small- and medium-size retailers to compete more effectively with department stores and large retail chains. The problems which have arisen because of competing bank charge plans should be mitigated to a large extent by a cooperative effort on the part of individual banks and joint-bank card ventures. Evidence indicates that many banks are taking steps to standardize their card plans and allow member merchants to maintain a relationship with *one* bank which will accept sales slips on the other banks. Development in the

[22] The survey taken in the Sixth Federal Reserve District indicated that less than 5 percent of the merchants participating as members in bank charge plans found that they could eliminate their own credit programs.

direction of standardization and cooperation among bank credit-card programs will depend on the initiative of the banking industry. Such initiative appears necessary if significant progress is to be made toward an electronic funds-transfer system.

For several years the large retailer will resist the bank credit card. The National Retail Merchants Association has indicated that many large retailers prefer having their own credit cards. They feel that the credit card gives them a direct link to the customer. One spokesman for Sears has stated, "We have an enormous credit card network of our own customers and we're not going to give it up without a fight." [23]

The feeling on the part of the managements of large retail chains that there is a "special bond" between the store and the customer who holds the store's credit card is the major objection these merchants have to participating in bank-card programs. This point was emphasized by a spokesman for the J. C. Penney Company; he stated that Penney's credit program "has some definite advantages to us. The kind of credit plans we offer, the criteria used for extending credit, the procedure for handling inquiries and adjustment policies are all under our control. We are in a position to make the credit decisions which we feel are best for our customers and best for the Penney Company. We believe this builds a special bond between our credit customers and the Penney store." [24]

The large retailer believes there are many other advantages to having a credit-card program. These advantages are not financial but rather marketing benefits. The retailer sees the customer's monthly charge statement as more than a request for payment; it is a monthly reminder of the relationship which exists between the cardholder and the store. The mailing of monthly statements presents an inexpensive means of distributing goodwill inserts, promotional material, and notices of special sales. The store's credit-cardholders provide the merchant with his own direct-mail list.

In addition, the retailer's credit-card system can provide management with important market-research information. When credit applications are filled out, management learns the customers' income levels, housing data, marital status, family characteristics, credit references, and other information. The large store also can compile statistics on how often customers shop at the store, what they buy, and how much they spend. In short, the large retailer with automated credit services can make

[23] "Electronic Money," *Forbes*, p. 44.
[24] Kenneth S. Axelson, Vice President/Director of Finance and Administration, J. C. Penney Company, Inc., New York. Presentation before the National Credit-Card Conference of the American Bankers Association, Chicago, Illinois, November 9, 1967.

extensive marketing use of its credit activities; it has a large investment in its credit department, and most important he feels that the store's *own* credit card establishes a bond between the store and the cardholder. The larger retailer feels that he would be sacrificing too much by participating in a bank credit plan, accepting the bank's credit card, which is also honored at competing establishments.

As bank credit-card plans become more sophisticated, it appears that banks will be able to offer the small- and medium-size retailer many of the marketing advantages currently enjoyed by the large retail merchants. Because of the benefits and the prevailing attitude of the larger retailers toward their own credit-card programs, it is expected that some time will elapse before these merchants become interested in bank credit plans. However, after several years' time and significant progress has been made toward an electronic funds-transfer system, the advantages of a single card and the attendant services offered by the commercial banking system should motivate the individual consumer to demand acceptance of his bank money card at all retail establishments.

8.7.2. Fully Implemented Electronic Funds-Transfer System. One of the most significant features of a future electronic funds-transfer system that will affect retailers is that the economies of scale in processing and extending credit will be available to all retailers, regardless of size and volume of sales. Naturally this feature will be most advantageous to small- and medium-size retailers. Thus, it is expected that the competitive position of these merchants will improve vis-à-vis the large department and chain stores.

Most smaller merchants and eventually many large merchants will welcome relief from the burden of operating their own credit systems. It was indicated in Chapter 5 that retail credit departments of even large stores cannot be justified in terms of profitability *per se*. The cost of extending credit must be passed on to customers in the form of higher prices throughout the retailing industry. With an electronic funds-transfer system, merchants will be able to compete more effectively in terms of prices, quality of merchandise, and service. Credit availability will no longer provide a method of competing for retail customers.

When sales are made, immediate deposit credit will be given to the vendor by the banking system, thus enabling the retailer to keep working capital to a minimum. Accounts receivable will be eliminated for the merchant, and the additional funds provided will make it possible for him to reduce his cost of capital or expand his operations. Banks will be in a position to offer many new services to their retail customers. The computerized information system will permit banks to handle a firm's basic accounting functions; manage its working capital, so as to minimize opportunity costs on idle balances; and provide analyses of financial data such as sales analysis, expense analysis, and inventory control.

On the basis of data triggered at point-of-sale terminals, information analyses will provide retail managements with valuable tools for operations control and more effective decision-making. The on-line system can be designed to tabulate daily sales figures, classified according to sales personnel, sales departments, product, time of day, or however desired. Terminal devices also could serve as sources of information for marketing research. With little difficulty, sales personnel could punch in data on a customer's approximate age, sex, reason for purchasing a product, or its planned use at the same time the sale is consummated.

In summary, under a future electronic funds-transfer system retailers will be relieved of the burden and costs of extending credit. Small- and medium-size merchants will be able to compete more effectively with large stores, and many new services and operating and marketing information will be available to all retailers. During the period of transition to the "cashless-checkless" society, however, banks will have to cooperate and standardize their respective credit programs in order to remove the inconveniences now experienced by participating merchants. Large retailers will be the last to engage in charge-account banking, but the pressures of consumers for the acceptance of a single money card and the economies and services offered by commercial banks eventually will force them to abandon their credit-card activities in favor of the electronic funds-transfer system.

**The Implications
of Electronic
Funds Transfer
for
Monetary Policy**   Chapter Nine

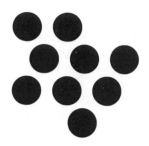

At the present time there is no single, generally accepted explanation of the relationships between financial variables and real economic activity. There is no general theory which adequately explains the process by which the initial impact of stabilization measures is transmitted to the total economic system and elicits certain types of responses from economic units in the consumer and business sectors. Economic theory has not kept pace with the dynamic changes occurring in the financial system; much analytical and theoretical research needs to be done in this area.

The purpose of this chapter is to analyze within a conceptual framework a few of the possible implications of innovation in the credit and payments mechanism for economic stabilization policies. The progression toward a future computerized monetary system will have dynamic effects on every segment of economic activity. This chapter will be limited to an analysis of implications within three broad areas; for purposes of organization, this treatment will consider the stabilization implications of (1) the effects of changes in monetary velocity and the demand for money, (2) the effects of changes in credit extension and the composition of financial assets, and (3) the effects of increased availability of economic data on the timing and efficacy of monetary policy.

9.1. The Effects of Changes in Monetary Velocity and the Demand for Money[1]

9.1.1. The Concept of Monetary Velocity. The essential functions which traditionally have served to identify what is "money" were discussed in Chapter 2. When a monetary medium is introduced into a barter system and there is no longer a need for a double coincidence of wants, a single transaction becomes separated into the distinct elements of sale and purchase. Not only are the transactions distinguished, but money separates the transactions in time. The time interval would be zero only when there existed a double coincidence of wants, and in such cases the need for money would be eliminated. Therefore, the

[1] Much of the foundation for this section is adapted with changes from D. W. Richardson, "The Potential Impact of Technical Innovations in Commercial Banking on the Transactions Demand for Money Balances," *Marquette Business Review*, Winter 1967, pp. 138–144.

general acceptability of money as a medium of exchange implicitly suggests that money will be held over time.

In our present economy money receipts in the form of income do not coincide exactly with patterns of money expenditures. Because of the time lag between payments and receipts, and receipts and expenditures, money necessarily must act as a store of value by virtue of its use as a medium of exchange. Money is actually used as a store of value to a much larger extent than as a medium of exchange.

The concept of monetary velocity refers to the degree of utilization of the money supply. It attempts to measure the rapidity with which the monetary unit is used in transacting purchases and sales over a given period of time. The higher the frequency of payments and receipts, the smaller the average balance required to finance a given level of economic activity. Theoretically, the transactions velocity of money can be calculated by dividing the number of dollar transactions by the average number of dollars owned by the public. Velocity is the result of the cumulative decisions of individuals and business firms with respect to the size of the money balances they choose to hold relative to their expenditure outlays.

9.1.2. The Concept of Demand for Money. As far back as 1917, A. C. Pigou stated that economic units hold idle sums of money and that the aggregate demand for money balances is a function of the rate of interest. The importance of the demand-for-money function in aggregate economic theory was emphasized by John Maynard Keynes in his iconoclastic work, *The General Theory of Employment, Interest and Money*, published in 1936. Even though the earlier Cambridge version of the quantity theory of money shifted analytical emphasis from the supply of money *per se* to the idea that people desire and need to hold money balances as such, it was Keynes who pushed the analysis more deeply into the reasons why economic units want to hold money.

Keynes's explanation in the *General Theory* through the development of the notion of *liquidity-preference* is generally accepted today by contemporary economists. From the development of liquidity-preference a theory of interest is constructed which provides the crucial link between money, income, and the employment level. Keynes used the term "liquidity-preference" to mean the demand to hold money balances; this concept forms the core of the modern analysis of money and its role in the economy.

Modern income and employment theory postulates three reasons why consumer units and business firms want to hold money balances: the transactions motive, the precautionary motive, and the speculative motive. The transactions motive relates to the demand to hold an average quantity of money balances in order to transact daily economic dealings. The transactions motive is primarily related to the medium-of-exchange function of money; it arises because the receipt of income by economic units is not synchronized exactly with all transactions involving money outlays.

The desire to hold some quantity of money to meet unforeseen contingencies is called the precautionary motive. Because individuals and business firms have incomplete knowledge of future events and in many cases no immediate access to highly liquid negotiable securities, a situation may arise in which the need for money is much greater than the amount required to carry on normal daily transactions.

The speculative motive relates to the desire to hold money balances in order to take advantage of future market movements. This motive shifts emphasis from the medium-of-exchange function of money to the store-of-value function. The individual or business firm holds money as an asset in preference to some other type of asset.

9.1.3. The Effect of Bank Innovations on Velocity and the Demand for Money. As was suggested earlier, and also pointed out by Keynes, in a simple economy the demand for money arises from two of money's functions: its use as a medium of exchange (transactions demand) and its use as a store of value (asset demand). Expectations of future changes in the rate of interest determine the asset-demand function of money. The transactions demand arises due to the failure of receipts and expenditures to be synchronized perfectly. It is possible to earn a return on transactions balances, however, by investing them in highly liquid interest-yielding assets and shifting into money only at the time an outlay is made. The square-root inventory formula for transactions demand based on this shiftability assumption has been advanced by Tobin and Baumol.[2] The disadvantage of such behavior, stated by Tobin, is the cost, pecuniary and nonpecuniary, of frequent and small transactions between money and other assets.[3] However, in analyses little attention is devoted to the nonpecuniary costs. For the average economic unit, such costs are represented by the time and effort required to transfer relatively small amounts of funds from a checking account to a savings account (or other asset) and back to a checking account at least once and perhaps several times during each income interval.

The advantage, of course, of shifting demand-deposit balances into other assets is the yield. The apparent interest inelasticity of transac-

[2] See James Tobin, "The Interest-Elasticity of Transactions Demand for Cash," *The Review of Economics and Statistics*, August 1956, pp. 241–246, and William J. Baumol, "The Transactions Demand for Cash: An Inventory Theoretic Approach," *The Quarterly Journal of Economics*, 1952, pp. 545–556.
[3] Tobin, *Review of Economics and Statistics*, p. 241.

tions demand for money balances on the part of household units and in many cases business firms would appear to be most closely associated with the nonpecuniary costs of shifting deposit balances. Only at extremely low rates of interest would pecuniary costs prohibit the temporary investment in a savings account or other highly liquid asset.

The three bank innovations which will have the greatest impact on velocity and the demand for money are (1) the bank credit card, (2) the automatic shifting of deposit balances by banks, and (3) the cash-advance feature of the bank credit card.

The impact on the use of money by the bank credit card can be seen by hypothesizing an economy where only money transactions take place. In such an economy, the consumer or business firm would have to have the necessary money balance in advance of each purchase. However, with the use of the bank credit card, the amount of currency in the hands of the public decreases and would be deposited presumably in individual checking accounts. The commercial banking system would pass on the additional currency to the Federal Reserve System, thus increasing bank reserves, which would permit a larger volume of deposits, loans, and investments. In short, everything else remaining the same, a transition from money to bank credit cards would be inflationary, necessitating the implementation of controls designed to limit monetary expansion.

For example, hypothesize an individual with a monthly income of one thousand dollars, mortgage payments of two hundred dollars, and other expenses of eight hundred dollars. His monthly account activity would show an initial deposit of one thousand dollars and a gradual withdrawal over the next thirty days, total debits equaling one thousand dollars. However, if all transactions were made with the use of a bank credit card, the first month would show no debits except for mortgage payment, two hundred dollars. At the end of the month, when the credit-card charges become due, the individual would have received his next monthly "paycheck" (preauthorized deposit from his employer). Because of the lag between the receipt of the product or service and the disbursement in payment, there would be an addition to the individual's stock of free capital of eight hundred dollars. At the same time, it would be unnecessary for the cardholder to withdraw money in the form of cash to make purchases. Thus the effect of a decrease in the amount of currency held by the public would increase bank reserves, and the use of the bank credit card would increase bank loans and deposits.

The automatic shifting of deposit balances by banks would remove the nonpecuniary costs of shifting idle money balances held because of the transactions and precautionary motives into some other liquid assets yielding interest income. In most cases banks will promote the shifting of excess demand-deposit balances into their own savings accounts. These shifts in deposit balances will have several effects that are important for economic stabilization policies. First, there will be a large reduction in demand-deposit balances in the banking system, and under a comprehensive direct funds-transfer system the transactions demand for money will approach zero. Under existing reserve requirements, a continual increase in savings and time-deposit balances will have the effect of increasing bank excess reserves and will permit a greater expansion of bank credit.

In essence the degree of efficiency of the money supply will increase (monetary velocity will increase), making it necessary for the monetary authorities to reduce the quantity of money in order to retain price stability. Looking at the whole economy, suppose national income were four hundred dollars per year; this income level could be achieved with a total quantity of money equal to one hundred dollars if transactions velocity were four. Of course, any number of combinations of M (money supply) and V (transactions velocity) could equal a four hundred-dollar Y (income), such that

$M =$	100	50	25	12 1/2	6 1/4	3 1/8	17/16	$\rightarrow 0$
$V =$	4	8	16	32	64	128	256	$\rightarrow \infty$

It becomes clear that theoretically any M which is greater than zero can produce a desired Y if V is allowed to vary. With V as the independent variable, over time the quantity of money becomes a function of velocity, $M = f(V)$; and so does the transactions demand for money balances $D_t = f(V_t)$. As monetary velocity increases due to institutional changes and innovations in the payments mechanism, it will become necessary for the monetary authorities to reassess their traditional definition of the money supply (which excludes time and savings deposits and other highly liquid financial assets), reevaluate reserve requirements on time and savings deposits, and perhaps implement new tools for control of monetary velocity.

In modern income and employment theory, by virtually common consent the transactions demand and precautionary demand for money have been taken as independent of monetary velocity. It has been common practice to lump the transactions and precautionary demands together since both are related closely to the medium-of-exchange function of money. Let the combined demand for money to satisfy the transactions and precautionary motives be called the *transactions de-*

mand and be designated by the symbol D_t. In post-Keynesian analysis the transactions demand (D_t) is assumed to be a function of the income level (Y) and the rate of interest (i), as illustrated in the accompanying diagram. It becomes apparent that when velocity is permitted to vary

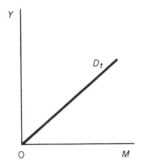
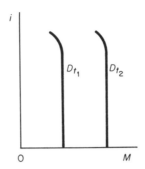

(as it is predicted to occur during the progression toward a future electronic funds-transfer system) the transactions demand becomes a function of the degree of efficiency of the money supply (e.g., transactions velocity) such that $MV = a$, as illustrated. The transactions de-

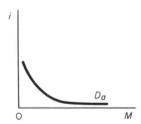

mand function takes the form of an equilateral hyperbola, $MV = a$, where a is a constant. The asset demand function (D_a) arising from the speculative motive for liquidity would take a form such that

$$M = a \operatorname{sech}^{-1} \frac{i}{a} - \sqrt{a^2 - i^2}, \text{ or}$$

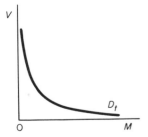

The foregoing argument should be strengthened by consideration of the third bank innovation previously referred to, namely, the cash-advance feature on the bank credit card. The bank credit-card cash advance, described in Chapter 6, permits the cardholder to make an immediate personal loan up to a stated limit (present limits range from three hundred to three hundred and fifty dollars). The immediate availability of what amounts to a net addition to a cardholder's demand-deposit balance upon request further mitigates his motivation to hold precautionary or even speculative money balances. The effect would be to put additional pressures on reductions in demand-deposit balances and currency held by the public.

9.2. The Effects of Changes in Credit Extension and the Composition of Financial Assets

9.2.1. Changes in Credit Extension. As bank credit cards increase in number and degree of utilization, there will be a general shift of the extension of consumer credit from the nonbanking sector of the economy to the banking sector. Not only will there be a shift in consumer credit but trade credit will be largely replaced with bank credit under an electronic funds-transfer system. Since bank credit is defined as money, the use of this credit for the financing of firms' receivables will have the tendency of putting additional pressures on increasing the quantity of money. During a period of general economic expansion the effect would be inflationary unless appropriate controls were used by the monetary authorities.

Those business firms which generally experience a positive net-accounts-receivable position (accounts receivable greater than accounts payable), it might be argued, would use their increased working capital to reduce some other forms of indebtedness. However, established financial-management practices would indicate that additional funds provided through the elimination of receivables and payables would be used for increasing investments. On the other hand, business firms with a negative net-accounts-receivable position (accounts receivable less than accounts payable) might find it necessary to increase their long-term indebtedness to improve their working capital position and current ratio. In either case it is expected that the results of substituting bank credit for trade credit would be expansionary and not restrictive.

Another factor which will tend to increase the commercial banking system's commitment to the consumer credit market is the fact that bank credit will be extended (through the bank credit card) to cover purchases from many firms that presently do not offer credit. Not only will credit sales be made from small merchants who cannot afford to offer credit, but bank credit cards will be used to make purchases of products and services which traditionally have not been offered on a credit basis.[4]

It is difficult to be very precise about the effect of credit availability on real economic activity since there is no accurate means of measuring availability. Interest rates may remain unchanged during the same period of time that banks change the ground rules as to who receives bank credit and how much.[5] Although monetary authorities effect stabilization policies to a large extent through measures which influence both the level and structure of interest rates, empirical studies have indicated that generally consumers are less responsive to changes in interest rates than business firms.[6] The interest inelasticity on the part of individuals would indicate that the effect of stabilization-policy measures operating through the rate of interest may be somewhat mitigated under an electronic funds-transfer system. The anticipated increase of bank credit held by consumers would suggest the necessity for the imposition of new policy tools aimed directly at controlling the availability of consumer credit.

At the present time, customers who fail to obtain credit oftentimes resort to the use of trade credit as a temporary source of financing.[7] With trade credit supplied by the banking system, it would be expected that business firms and individuals would seek accommodation through their respective banks. In periods of tight money, individuals could make extensive use of the cash-advance feature of their bank money cards. With existing lines of credit on bank credit cards ranging around three hundred dollars, and with an anticipated eighty to ninety million money-card accounts under the electronic funds-transfer system, the commercial banking system could be faced with severe liquidity problems if a majority of the cardholders exercised their "overdraft" privileges. If money were already tight, banks would have to seek adjustments in their reserve positions by borrowing from the Federal Reserve System. In a case such as the one just described, policy measures taken to increase the rate of interest might well intensify the use of preauthorized lines of credit. Customers who found it more difficult to

---

[4] At the present time such establishments as grocery stores, supermarkets, beauty shops, and laundry and dry-cleaning establishments are participating as members of bank credit card plans.

[5] For a theoretical treatment of the aggregate economic implications of credit rationing, see Robert Shapiro, "Financial Intermediaries, Credit Availability, and Aggregate Demand," *Journal of Finance*, September 1966, pp. 459–475.

[6] Exceptions would include mortgage credit and to a lesser extent automobile installment credit.

[7] Allan H. Meltzer, "Monetary Policy and the Trade Credit Practices of Business Firms," in *Stabilization Policies*, Commission on Money and Credit (Englewood Cliffs, N.J.: Prentice-Hall, 1963), pp. 471–497.

obtain loanable funds from other sources due to increased rates of interest could rely on their money cards for cash advances. Again, this situation would tend to emphasize the need for more direct controls by the monetary authorities over the extension of credit.

9.2.2. Changes in the Composition of Financial Assets. One of the innovations previously discussed under an electronic funds-transfer system is the automatic shifting of demand-deposit balances by commercial banks in accordance with the preauthorized investment portfolios of customers. It was pointed out that banks will tend to promote shifts of excess balances into those financial assets which will be most beneficial for the banks—namely, commercial bank savings and time deposits. The implications of future changes in the composition of bank deposits were discussed in Chapter 8. Once a customer's savings account reaches a desired limit, however, demand-deposit shifts will be made into higher-yielding financial assets.

At the present time, several of the large banks have or are in the process of obtaining interests in mutual funds into which customers' excess deposit balances can be invested. Whether or not this trend will increase will depend upon legal and regulatory developments.[8] It would appear safe to assume, however, that progression toward the "cashless-checkless" society will result in a much "closer association" between the commercial banking industry and many nonbank financial intermediaries. The net result of automatic, preauthorized investments would be a general shift away from money to "near-money" assets held by the public.

A more unified financial structure and greater emphasis on near-money assets would undoubtedly give added credence to two arguments that are receiving increased attention in current economic and financial literature. These are (1) there is a need to reevaluate the traditional definition of the money supply; and (2) there is a need for greater regulation of nonbank financial intermediaries in order to make monetary policy more effective.[9]

[8] Recall (Chapter 3) that investment interests were ordered divorced from commercial banks with the passage of the Banking Act of 1933; however, recent liberal interpretations of the law (Chapter 6) have allowed banks to own corporate stock, "when such ownership is a proper incident to banking."
[9] See John G. Gurley and Edward S. Shaw, *Money in a Theory of Finance* (Washington, D.C.: The Brookings Institution, 1960); Donald Shelby, "Some Implications of the Growth of Financial Intermediaries," *Journal of Finance,* December 1958, pp. 527–541; Richard S. Thorn, "Nonbank Financial Intermediaries, Credit Expansion, and Monetary Policy," *Staff Papers,* International Monetary Fund, VI (November 1958), 369–383; and Eugene A. Birnbaum, "The Growth of Financial Intermediaries as a Factor in the Effectiveness of Monetary Policy," *Staff Papers,* International Monetary Fund, VI (November 1958), pp. 384–426.

At the present time, the expansion of near-money assets is dependent to a great extent upon the concurrent level of expansion in the stock of money. The motivation for economic units to shift funds from demand-deposit accounts to near-money assets is the yield, but the exchange process is limited by the costs (pecuniary and nonpecuniary) and the need to hold minimum cash balances for transactions purposes. However, as was emphasized earlier, under an electronic funds-transfer system transactions balances will be greatly reduced (if not eliminated) and the nonpecuniary costs of funds transfers will be eliminated. Pecuniary costs will be represented by charges made by commercial banks in the form of fees for making deposit transfers and service charges for setting up and maintaining customers' investment portfolios.

When demand deposits are used to purchase the liabilities of financial intermediaries, the ownership of the demand-deposit balances is shifted from the previous owner to the intermediary. The institution retains a small portion of the deposits for reserves and transfers the funds to other economic units. Even though the stock of money remains unchanged, additional highly liquid assets are created. The result is a pyramiding effect that adds additional leverage to stabilization measures that effect changes in the money supply. According to the Chairman of the Board of Governors of the Federal Reserve System, the effect of an expansion in near-money assets would be inflationary. He stated that

The "near-money" nature of the liabilities of various nonbank financial institutions may induce holders of these liabilities to spend more freely out of current incomes than they would if the liabilities they held had a greater degree of risk. This would be true also if savers held short-term marketable Government securities or other liquid assets of this type. As a consequence, changes in the public's holdings of such liquid assets need to be taken into consideration in determining credit and monetary policies directed toward maintaining a supply of money appropriate for sustained growth.[10]

Any inflationary pressures brought about by the expansion of near-money assets could be curbed by stabilization measures aimed at reducing the stock of money. It may be argued therefore that nonbank financial intermediaries are subject to the same credit restraints limiting all bank credit expansion. To an increasing extent, however, the position of nonbank financial intermediaries will be one of greatly affecting the velocity or rate of utilization of the existing money supply. This gives rise to another well-debated issue, that is, whether the com-

[10] United States Joint Economic Committee, *Employment, Growth, and Price Levels, Hearings* Part 6C, 86th Congress, 1st Session (Washington, D.C.: Government Printing Office, 1959).

mercial-banking system should continue to be required to assume an undue share of the burden associated with stabilization policies. As commercial banks become more heavily committed in the high-volume, low-margin consumer-loan market, it would be expected that the banking system would become more vulnerable to adverse reactions from stabilization policies. Such a position would provide added argumentation for the imposition of reserve requirements or some other forms of regulation on nonbank intermediaries.

9.3. The Availability of Economic Data and Its Effects on the Timing and Efficacy of Monetary Policy

There has been much debate during the last two decades concerning the effectiveness of economic stabilization measures and the proper mix between monetary and fiscal policies. It is not the purpose of this treatise to analyze policy objectives and the relative merits of monetary and fiscal measures. This section primarily will be concerned with the impact of innovation in the credit and payments mechanism on the timing and efficacy of existing monetary policies directed toward economic stabilization. The analysis of the impact of innovation on monetary policy will be limited to changes that may result in the structural and institutional constraints to policy measures.[11]

The major institutional constraint on monetary policy can be identified as a series of lags in its implementation. While the actual evidence concerning lags is scant, there is general agreement that a lack of timing is a major factor mitigating the efficacy of monetary policy. The Commission on Money and Credit concluded that general monetary controls since World War II have required from six to nine months to produce a change in the direction of ease, and a further six months for their maximum effect.[12] Professor Milton Friedman has taken the position that the lags are so long and so variable that monetary policy does not necessarily stabilize but may as often contribute to the violence of economic fluctuations.[13]

The first lag, often referred to as the "recognition lag," represents the lapse of time between the moment when there is a need for a change in policy and the moment the monetary authorities recognize

[11] For an excellent summary of the limitations of monetary policy that are thought to be of a general theoretical nature see James R. Schlesinger, "Monetary Policy and Its Critics," *Journal of Political Economy*, December 1960, pp. 601–616.

[12] *Money and Credit: Their Influence on Jobs, Prices, and Growth,* The Report of the Commission on Money and Credit (Englewood Cliffs, N.J. Prentice-Hall, 1961), p. 49.

[13] Milton Friedman, *A Program for Monetary Stability* (New York; Fordham University Press, 1960), p. 87.

the need. Second,[14] there is a lag between the moment when an action is taken by the monetary authorities and the moment when the banking system begins to be faced with changed conditions. And third, even after business firms and household units are confronted with a changed supply of money and credit, there is an inevitable lag before real output can be affected.[15]

It would appear reasonable to assume that the recognition lag will be shortened considerably under the electronic funds-transfer system. The national network of regional computer centers virtually will become a storehouse of information on prices, interest rates, monetary velocity, number and kind of retail sales, wholesale purchases, intercompany deposit transfers, security sales, tax data, and a vast number of other areas. These data will be available instantaneously to the monetary and fiscal authorities. Because the Federal Reserve System and the Treasury will have their own computer facilities and be on an on-line relationship with the regional computer centers, data may be programed to provide information classified by geographical regions, major money market centers, Federal Reserve districts, size of bank, type of data, or however desired.

Not only will the application of what might be called "monetary cybernetics" serve to reduce the recognition lag, it will provide new kinds of information heretofore not available in any form. Because of the quality and quantity of data that will be available, the entire lag problem may be eliminated by the development of new economic forecasting techniques. In large measure, due to a current lack of financial and economic data, the monetary authorities have tended to avoid prognostication. The problem has been described by two former members of the staff of the Federal Reserve System:

There exists in the Federal Reserve System an unwritten rule against explicit forecasting of business conditions; even modest attempts at prognosis are blue-penciled if written and ignored if expressed verbally. Members of the FOMC [Federal Open Market Committee] often remark that "we are making policy only for the next 3 weeks," the implication being that inaction or wrong action can be reviewed or corrected at the next meeting. Now it is manifestly impossible to frame an intelligent monetary policy without at least implicit forecasting. . . . Fortunately, many FOMC members have their own unstated projections. But the emphasis on the short term, the avoidance of a solid, common forecast, and the frequency of FOMC meetings all lead to

[14] There will also be a short time lapse between "recognition" and action; however, this lag is relatively short since the Federal Open Market Committee meets often — generally every three weeks.
[15] See John Kareken and Robert M. Solow, "Lags in Monetary Policy: A Summary," in *Stabilization Policies*, pp. 3–7.

erratic action, lagged responses, and policy more often than not based on correction of past errors rather than on anticipation of future events.[16]

The availability of data under the electronic funds-transfer system will not only permit the development of accurate forecasting techniques but will also provide a more accurate basis for effective decision-making and review and control techniques. In short, it is expected that the quality and availability of economic data under the electronic funds-transfer system will improve immensely the timing and efficacy of existing stabilization measures. It should be emphasized, however, that the projected innovations in the credit and payments mechanism and their effects on the monetary system will require much research, new approaches, and enlightened attitudes toward the new roles of "money" and credit in society and the economy.

[16] Delbert C. Hastings and Ross M. Robertson, "The Mysterious World of the Fed," *Business Horizons,* Spring 1962.

**Summary
and
Conclusions**

Chapter Ten

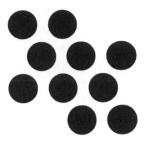

The concept of "money" never has been clearly defined, nor can it be. Money can be described only in terms of the functions it performs. The record of history has demonstrated clearly that the things that evolved to serve the functions of money were highly imbued with mystical, religious, sociological, and psychological attributes that greatly influenced the utilitarian operations of money in society. In more recent history money has become more and more a "concept" and less and less a "thing"; however, society's attitude toward money and the ways in which it is used continues to be an important factor to consider in an analysis of innovation in payment media.

To date there have been only four major innovations in payment-media systems; the United States has experimented with all four. The federal government's power to coin and regulate the value of money has been implicitly delegated to the Federal Reserve System and the commercial-banking industry. Today, approximately 80 percent of the money supply is in the form of demand-deposit balances in commercial banks. Transfers of these balances, for the most part, are consummated with the use of checks.

The check-clearing procedure has evolved into a cumbersome process largely influenced by habit and tradition. Last year Americans wrote over eighteen billion checks with a value of approximately four trillion dollars, and these figures are increasing at the rate of 6 to 7 percent annually. The costs per year to the banking system alone of handling and physically transporting checks from payees to payors and banks to banks is estimated to be nearly three and one-half billion dollars. Individuals occupy the central and most important position in the check-writing, check-receiving process. Nearly 60 percent of the checks written by individuals are sent through the mail, putting a great amount of pressure on an already overburdened postal service.

10.1. The Role of Credit and the Credit Card

The large increase in consumer credit since World War II has had the effect of stimulating economic activity and increasing the number of transactions; however, credit has fostered a less than proportionate increase in the number of checks written per volume of transactions.

Several debts incurred through credit transactions can be discharged with a single payment in money. Of the many devices which have developed to facilitate the use of credit, the credit card has been the most significant. In fact, the largest single category of checks written by individuals and sent through the mail is for payments for charges incurred by credit cards.

At the retail level the credit card has become the major device used for the substitution of credit for cash and checks. Not only have private credit-card companies emerged, which now number their memberships in the hundreds of thousands, but most large retailers and petroleum companies issue their own credit cards. Businessmen make extensive use of travel and entertainment credit cards. These cards primarily are used to make purchases of goods and services from motels, hotels, clubs, restaurants, and transportation firms. Originally, petroleum-company credit cards were used exclusively for the purchase of gasoline and automotive accessories, but in recent years the oil industry has expanded the use of its credit cards into the travel and entertainment credit market. Largely due to the great number of outstanding credit cards which are considered "inactive," petroleum companies have attempted to stimulate card usage by merchandising schemes offering a wide range of goods having no relationship to the petroleum industry. Many problems associated with credit cards have developed, such as a manifestation of Gresham's Law, counterfeiting, and kiting — concepts which traditionally have been reserved for monetary instruments.

Nearly three-quarters of all American families hold credit cards or have charge accounts. Typically, an average middle-class family may hold upwards of a dozen credit cards and have established charge accounts with several retailers. Department stores are the major issuers of "single-establishment" credit cards; these are cards that may be used to make purchases from only the issuing institution. Charge accounts are offered by most retailers as a means of attracting customers and increasing sales revenue; they cannot be justified in terms of costs and profits alone. Many medium- and small-size retailers cannot afford to offer charge-account services, even though the American consumer has come to demand and expect the extension of retail credit, and it is these retailers who make up the bulk of the retail multiple-establishment credit-card market.

10.2. Advent of the Bank Credit Card

In large measure, due to the unfavorable competitive position of the smaller retail merchant who could not afford to offer credit, "charge-account" banking developed as a means of substituting bank credit for retail credit. The first commercial-bank credit card was issued by the

Franklin National Bank of New York in 1952. At that time most commercial banks were not interested in entering what had been traditionally a small-size, low-margin loan market. In the late 1950s and early 1960s, however, the advent of computer and electronic data-processing technology provided a means by which the consumer credit market could prove very lucrative to the commercial-banking industry. As is the case with any low-margin product, the key to profitability is volume, and the technical equipment which was made available in the later 1950s made it economically feasible for a commercial bank to handle a large volume of credit-card transactions.

The large initial investment and high fixed costs associated with electronic data-processing equipment were not undertaken by banks with the primary intention of issuing credit cards and entering a new market that was looked upon by most bankers skeptically as an extremely risky venture. During this time many large banks, particularly in California, found themselves in a position where they were forced to automate their demand-deposit operations because of staffing problems and increased costs. Once having obtained automation equipment, however, banks sought other profitable applications of their computer capabilities. Among these services were bank credit cards and preauthorized payments.

The initial entry and success of several large bank credit-card programs (particularly the Bank of America) led commercial banks by the hundreds in the mid-1960s to initiate credit-card services. Favorable interpretation of the Banking Act of 1933 by the Comptroller of the Currency removed any threat of legal restraint on nationally chartered banks' entry into the credit-card field. By January 1968, it was estimated that about 1,400 commercial banks were offering some sort of credit card.

10.3. A "Moneyless" Society

The gradual acceptance of preauthorized payment plans, the widespread use of bank credit cards, and the advent of more highly sophisticated computer and electronic data-processing technology recently have led to many bankers' speculations of a future "cashless-checkless" society. It would be theoretically feasible for even an advanced economy to exist without a medium of exchange, as the concept is known today. A money of account would be needed to provide a common denominator by which to measure value and prices; however, money would not need to exist in any material form. Transactions could be consummated through a nationwide, computerized system for offsetting debts and credits.

A close analysis of the present-day commercial-banking system reveals that the banking industry performs the function of a dealer in debts which offsets debts and credits through an elaborate and, in many ways, cumbersome institutional framework involving a wide range of instruments. Because of the confidence and general acceptability of some of these instruments as media of exchange, they have come to be defined as money. The elimination of what is now used as money could be achieved with the implementation of an electronic funds-transfer system. Such a system would consist of two hundred to three hundred regional computer centers with each regional center on an on-line, real-time relationship with each bank and retailer in its region.

10.4. A Future Electronic Funds-Transfer System

Electronic funds transfers would be initiated at points of sale by the insertion of bank money cards into remote terminal devices located in merchants' establishments. The operation would be very similar to the use of existing bank credit cards except that computer automation and high-speed communications technology would eliminate all paperwork and the time required to process sales tickets, monthly bills, and other paper. The money card would permit funds to be transferred instantly from payor to payee, or the bank could credit the merchant's account immediately and create a loan to the cardholder.

It would appear reasonable that electronic funds transference is a logical extension of traditional commercial-bank functions and that its future implementation seems assured because of its inherent economies and convenience and because of the increasing pressure to find means of coping with the growing volume of paper surrounding the present debt-settlement process. It is not inevitable, however, that the commercial-banking industry will occupy the pivotal position in a future electronic funds-transfer system.

In certain areas of the country, competition among various bank credit-card plans has led to (1) the unsolicited issuance of bank credit cards; (2) issuance of bank credit cards to poor credit risks; (3) lost, stolen, and misused cards; and (4) increased merchant dissatisfaction. Unless there is a cooperative effort on the part of the commercial-banking industry to solve these problems in the near future, it will become increasingly difficult to sell individuals and merchants on an electronic funds-transfer system.

The most likely direction for progression toward a future "cashless-checkless" society will be that which involves the least amount of change in habits and customs. When the Bank of America first introduced its bank card, it was advertised as a "family credit-card service" (instead of a "BankAmericard") because it was believed that consumer acceptance would be greater if the bank's credit card appeared little different from other credit cards with which individuals already were familiar. Once the bank's credit card was accepted, it was promoted as a "BankAmericard." In short, the acceptance of a money card and the entire electronic funds-transfer concept will be much easier if there is general acceptance and satisfaction with the bank credit card on the part of both the consumer and the retailer.

10.5. The Implications of Electronic Funds Transference for Commercial-Banking and Other Industries

Progression toward a future electronic funds-transfer system will occasion changes in both bank management policies and the banking structure. Individual banks increasingly will feel the need to acquire computer capabilities and technically trained personnel. Small- and many medium-size banks will have to participate in cooperative ventures on a time-sharing basis in order to compete with the larger banks. Many bankers will need to engage in educational programs and develop new attitudes toward their changing role in the financial community. The character of the commercial bank will turn more to that of a service organization, making it necessary for management to become more concerned with marketing and public relations.

A larger share of bank profits will depend on service charges, and a reduction in demand deposits will cause banks to lose a major source of interest-free funds. The level of savings accounts will continue to rise, but so will their activity, making the traditional definition of the money supply increasingly obsolete. In view of the banks' central position in the payments mechanism, it would seem logical for the banking industry to increase its activities substantially beyond the accounting for debt settlement. Increasingly, for its commercial customers the banking industry will be in a position to perform the accounting and financing of receivables, billing and collecting operations, cash flow management, and financial planning.

By virtue of the money card and the other new services offered by commercial banks, the competitive position of the small- and medium-size retailer will greatly improve. At the present time the large department and chain stores that offer their own credit cards are not interested in participating in bank credit-card plans. Even though nearly all retail credit departments fail to make a profit on their credit activities, major retailers feel that they receive many marketing benefits from having their own credit-card operations. It is expected, however, that eventually large retailers will reluctantly join bank card programs because the consumer will demand the convenience of having only one card and one monthly bill.

Many industries will be affected by the movement toward a "cashless-checkless" society. Of the nonbank financial intermediaries, commercial finance and factoring companies and small-loan companies will find the commercial banking industry's innovations a serious threat to their survival. Savings banks and savings and loan associations appear to pose the greatest potential competition to the commercial banks. At the present time there is little threat because the savings-bank industry is relatively small and the savings and loan associations are severely restricted on their lending powers. The passage of the Federal Charter bill currently before the Congress, however, could provide the legal framework for the integration of the savings bank and savings and loan industries into a national system of federally chartered savings banks. Such a system could offer a broad range of financial services and compete aggressively with the commercial-banking industry for the predominant position in the electronic funds-transfer system.

10.6. The Implications of Electronic Funds Transference for Monetary Policy

The future use of bank money cards for consummating nearly all transactions will have the effect of eliminating the need for transactions balances in the form of both cash outside of banks and demand-deposit balances held in banks. Such a phenomenon would be expansionary in the long run, for cash would be passed on to the Federal Reserve System, adding to bank reserves; and excess demand-deposit balances would be shifted into savings and time deposits, which have lower reserve requirements.

During the progression toward an electronic funds-transfer system, monetary velocity will increase, and the supply of money (as it is currently defined) relative to economic activity will actually decrease. The cash-advance feature on bank credit cards (and eventually on money cards) will tend to reduce the precautionary demand for money. As individuals and business firms become more concerned about the time value of money, the transactions and precautionary demands for money may even become negative, especially during periods of inflation and high levels of interest rates. Over time the transactions demand will become less and less a function of the income level and interest rate. The level of transactions balances will depend on monetary velocity, which in turn will be determined by the rate of implementation of computer technology to the payments mechanism. It will become increasingly important for the monetary authorities to develop new policy tools directed at control of velocity and the availability of credit.

The extension of short-term credit by the banking system will increase greatly. Not only will short-term consumer credit increase, but a large portion of trade credit will be replaced by bank credit. Policy measures directed toward ease may have a greater impact on the business sector, but the "overdraft" privileges extended to individuals presumably would be exercised when consumers found it difficult to find loan accommodation elsewhere. If a large portion of the money cardholders made use of cash advances, the banking system would be faced with severe liquidity problems and there may be little restriction of aggregate demand.

Because it is expected that innovations in the credit and payments mechanism will lead to increased integration of financial institutions, there will be added credence to the so-called Gurley-Shaw thesis. Increased volatility of savings and time deposits coupled with a general rise in the level of other near-money assets will force the traditional definition of the money supply into obscurity.

The efficacy of monetary policy directed toward economic stabilization will be greatly improved under a fully implemented electronic funds-transfer system. The time lags that presently restrain monetary policy from being a much-needed tool for the construction of flexible, quick-acting stabilization measures may be largely reduced if not eliminated. Because the national system of regional computer centers will be able to provide instaneous data on nearly every vital segment of the economy, "monetary cybernetics" will permit the development of short-run fore-casting and review-and-control techniques not available at the present time.

Giro   Appendix 1
Credit-Transfer
Systems

The word "giro" was derived from the Greek "guros," meaning ring, circle, or circuit. A giro credit-transfer system is a financial system in which credit circulation takes the place of checks, banknotes, and coins. The basic difference between a giro system and a check system is that the payor initiates the credit transfer by ordering the bank or financial institution to credit the payee's account directly, thus eliminating much of the usual check-clearing process.

Today, most giro systems are conducted by postal authorities and are referred to as postal giro systems or post-office credit-transfer systems. In 1883, Emperor Franz Josef of Austria inaugurated a Post Office Savings Bank, and the bank's director, Dr. Georg Coch, introduced a credit-transfer system. Similar systems have been organized in every Western European country with the exception of Eire, Greece, Iceland, Portugal, Spain, Turkey, and the United Kingdom. Great Britain proposed the establishment of a postal giro system that was scheduled to be fully implemented in 1970.

The importance of the concept of a giro credit-transfer system to the present study is that it is a form of "checkless" banking. The main purpose of the giro system is to facilitate the transference of a high volume of small money balances. At the present time it is precisely this kind of business that is least profitable and most expensive for the commercial-banking industry.

A great importance of the giro concept is that it appears ready made for the latest developments in computer and electronic data-processing technology. The British system is to be completely computerized from its inception. To this end, the postal authorities invested over eight million dollars for computer equipment, and it will employ over three thousand new personnel.

A future electronic funds-transfer system operated by the United States commercial-banking system will employ many of the techniques

Sources: F. P. Thomson, *Giro Credit Transfer Systems* (Oxford: Pergamon Press, 1964); "The Giro, the Computer, and Checkless Banking," *Monthly Review* of the Federal Reserve Bank of Richmond, April 1966; and "World-Wide Expansion of the Giro System," *Burroughs Clearing House*, October 1966.

and practices currently used by giro credit-transfer systems. It is interesting to note that at the present time international credit transfers between Western European systems is commonplace. Many of these countries are linked by reciprocal agreements, such as the Universal Postal Union and the Nordic Post Giro Agreement. The European Economic Community is now considering further expansion of the giro concept to facilitate trade among participating nations.

May 12, 1933. The Thomas Inflation Amendment to the Agricultural Adjustment Act of 1933 authorized the President to revalue the silver dollar, to provide for unlimited coinage of silver at a fixed ratio with gold, and to accept limited quantities of silver from foreign countries in payment on war debts.

December 1933. The President directed the mint to purchase newly mined domestic silver at $1.29 a fine ounce, less a seigniorage charge of 50 percent. The net result was a "price" to the miners of 64.64+ cents per fine ounce.

June 19, 1934. The Silver Purchase Act of 1934 ruled it to be the policy of the United States that the metallic reserves of the country consist of 25 percent silver and 75 percent gold. The Secretary of the Treasury was directed to purchase both domestic and foreign silver at not more than $1.29 per ounce and not more than 50 cents per ounce for silver stocks existing in the country on May 1, 1934. The Secretary was permitted to sell silver in the world market if the price should go over $1.29.

July 6, 1939. The Act of July 6, 1939, directed the Secretary of the Treasury to buy at a price of 71.11 cents per fine ounce all silver offered by domestic miners.

July 31, 1946. The Act of July 31, 1946, increased the price at which the Treasury was directed to buy newly mined domestic silver to 90.5 cents per ounce.

November 28, 1961. The President directed the Treasury to discontinue sales of "free silver," to suspend its use for coinage, and to release silver through the retirement of $5 and $10 silver certificates.

June 4, 1963. Congress repealed the Silver Purchase Act, authorized the issuance of $1 and $2 Federal Reserve notes to replace silver certificates of the same denominations, directed the Secretary of the Treasury not to sell "free silver" for less than $1.2929 per ounce, and required the Secretary to exchange either silver dollars or silver bullion (at his discretion) for silver certificates when presented.

March 1964. The Treasury announced that it would redeem silver certificates only in silver bullion.

July 23, 1965.   The President signed the Coinage Act of 1965, providing for the coinage of silverless dimes and quarters and for reducing the silver content of half-dollars from 90% of gross weight to 40%. The act prohibited the minting of silver dollars for five years, and directed the Secretary of the Treasury to buy newly mined silver at $1.25 per ounce and to sell silver in excess of the reserves held against silver certificates at not less than $1.2929 per ounce. The Secretary was also authorized to prohibit the exporting or melting of United States coins. In addition, the act provided for the creation of a Joint Commission on Coinage to consist of 24 members to advise the President, the Secretary of the Treasury, and the Congress on matters of coinage.

May 1, 1967.   The President announced the appointment of the eight public members of the Joint Commission on Coinage; one of the Commission's tasks was to recommend the time when the Treasury should cease to maintain the price of silver at $1.2929.

May 18, 1967.   The Secretary of the Treasury exercised his authority under the Coinage Act of 1965 prohibiting the exportation and melting of United States coins.

June 24, 1968.   After twelve o'clock noon, Monday, June 24, 1968, the Treasury ceased redeeming silver certificates in silver.

Federal Reserve Notes

METHOD OF ISSUE. Issued through local Federal Reserve agents on request of local Federal Reserve Bank to agent.

RESERVE. Secured by a like amount of eligible discounted or purchased paper, or direct Federal Government obligations.

Silver Certificates

METHOD OF ISSUE. Issued by the Treasury and placed in circulation through the Federal Reserve Banks. Provision has been made for the gradual retirement of these certificates and their replacement by Federal Reserve Notes.

RESERVE. Silver bullion or silver dollars of equal monetary value.

United States Notes

METHOD OF ISSUE. New notes may be issued by the Treasury to replace worn-out notes, but the total amount outstanding may not be increased above $347 million.

RESERVE. $156 million of gold bullion (which includes gold backing for Treasury notes of 1890).

Treasury Notes of 1890

METHOD OF ISSUE. No new notes may be issued. Currently being retired on receipt.

RESERVE. Silver bullion or silver dollars of equal monetary value. Also shares reserve of $156 million of gold bullion with United States Notes.

Federal Reserve Bank Notes

METHOD OF ISSUE. No new notes may be issued. In process of retirement.

RESERVE. Deposits of lawful money of equal monetary value to redeem outstanding notes. When last authorized to be issued, the reserve was (a) any direct obligation of the United States or (b) any notes, drafts, bills of exchange, or banker's acceptances acquired by the Federal Reserve Banks.

National Bank Notes

METHOD OF ISSUE. No new notes may be issued. In process of retirement.

RESERVE. Deposits of lawful money of equal monetary value to redeem outstanding notes.

Gold Certificates

METHOD OF ISSUE. Issued by the Treasury and paid to Federal Reserve Banks only. These certificates are not permitted to enter the currency circulation of the country. The small amount now shown as outstand-

Source: *Readings on Money*, The Federal Reserve Bank of Richmond, 1963, with revisions by the writer to reflect subsequent developments.

ing is overhand from pre-1934 days, when gold coins and certificates circulated freely.

RESERVE.   Gold bullion of equal monetary value.

Standard Silver Dollars

METHOD OF ISSUE.   Issued by the Treasury and paid to Federal Reserve Banks in lieu of silver certificates if desired. None have been coined since 1935.

RESERVE.   No reserve. Total weight of coin is 412.5 grains, 90 percent silver and 10 percent copper alloy.

Subsidiary Silver Coins

METHOD OF ISSUE.   No new coins of this type are being issued. In process of retirement.

RESERVES.   No reserve. The weights of the coins (which are 90 percent silver and 10 percent copper alloy) are half-dollar, 192.9 grains; quarter, 96.45 grains; dime, 38.58 grains.

New Subsidiary Coins

METHOD OF ISSUE.   Issued by the Treasury and paid to Federal Reserve Banks to accommodate public demand and replace silver coins.

RESERVE.   No reserve. Passage of the Coinage Act of 1965 provided for the coinage of silverless dimes and quarters and for reducing the silver content of the half-dollar from 90 percent of gross weight to 40 percent. The half-dollar was to have a core composed of 79 percent copper and 21 percent silver "sandwiched" between facing layers composed of 20 percent copper and 80 percent silver. The quarters and dimes were to have a copper core "sandwiched" between facing layers composed of 75 percent copper and 25 percent nickel.

Minor Coins

METHOD OF ISSUE.   Issued by the Treasury and paid to Federal Reserve Banks to accommodate public demand.

RESERVE.   No reserve. Nickel: 77.16 grains, 75 percent copper and 25 percent nickel; penny: 48 grains, 95 percent copper and 5 percent tin or zinc.

American Oil Co.   Accounts 5.5 million; cards 8.5 million, 3 years. Inactive 50 percent accounts (no balance outstanding). Terms 3–12 months.
CHARGES: hotel/motel, car rental, some parts and services insurance, motor club membership, travel service, merchandise.
EXCHANGES: Humble, Imperial, Sohio, Standard of Calif.

American Petrofina Co. of Texas.   Accounts 280,000; cards 560,000, 3 years. Inactive 65 percent cards, 54 percent accounts (no purchases for 12 months). Terms to 6 months, no charges; 6–12 months, 5 percent.
CHARGES: installed TBA, lubrication, washing, wheel balancing, related services.
EXCHANGES: Canadian Petrofina, Tidewater.

Ashland Oil & Refining Co.   Nonexpiring cards. Terms, $20, 3 months; $50, 6 months; 12 months at 6 percent.
CHARGES: TBA, antifreeze, washing, lubrication.
EXCHANGES: Crown, Lion Supertest, Tenneco.

Atlantic Richfield Co., Atlantic Division.   Accounts 1 million; cards 1.6 million, 3 years and life. Inactive accounts 60 percent (owed no balance December 1966.) Terms $20–$50 3 months; over $50 6 months.
CHARGES: TBA, minor repairs, hotel/motel, car rental, baseball tickets.
EXCHANGES: Marathon, Pure, Sunray DX, Canadian Petrofina, Supertest, Irving, Skelly.

Richfield Division.   Cards 4 months and life.
CHARGES: TBA and some services.
EXCHANGES: Citgo, Sunray DX, Husky, Marathon, Sinclair, Skelly, British American, Supertest.

Champlin Petroleum Co.   Accounts 51,149; cards 212,539, 2 years. Inactive, cards 75 percent, accounts 5 percent (preceding month). Terms $30–$50, 3 months; over $50, 6 months.
CHARGES: TBS, minor repairs.
EXCHANGES: Honors all others, dealer pays 6% charge.

Chevron Oil Co., Eastern Division.   Accounts 170,000; cards 3 or 12 months. Terms: 3, 6, 9, 12 months.
CHARGES: TBA, repairs to $50, Ramada Inn, car rental.
EXCHANGES: Signal, Sohio, Fleetwing, Boron, Irving, Fina, Sunray DX, Phillips.

Chevron Oil Co., Western Division.   Accounts 300,000; cards 500,000, 3 and 12 months. Inactive accounts 46 percent (no purchases during current billing month); terms 3, 6, 9, 12 months.

Source: "Breakdown of Oil-Company Credit-Card Accounts," *1967 National Petroleum News Factbook Issue,* mid-May 1967.

CHARGES: TBA, minor repairs.
EXCHANGES: American, Sunray DX, Imperial, Irving, Sohio, Humble, Standard of Calif.

Cities Service Oil Co. Accounts 1.5 million, cards 2.3 million, life. Inactive accounts 51 percent (no purchase last 12 months). Terms: 6 months, $35 minimum no charge; 12 months over $75, $2.50 charge; over $100, $3.50 charge.
CHARGES: TBA, tune-ups, minor repairs, insurance, special merchandise.
EXCHANGES: Richfield, Sunray DX, British American, British Petroleum, Irving, Supertest, Humble.
UNIVERSAL CARDS: Diners Club, Carte Blanche, Chicago Bank Plan, various charges paid by company.

Consumer Service Stations. Accounts 30,000, cards 40,000; 24 months. Terms 6 months.
CHARGES: none but oil products.
EXCHANGES: none.

Continental Oil Co. Accounts 950,000; cards 2.9 million, 12 months and life. Inactive accounts 49 percent (no purchase in last 12 months). Terms 3, 6, 12 months for TBA; 12 months for travel.
CHARGES: TBA, labor, repairs, hotel.
EXCHANGES: Shell, Union, Shell Canada, White Rose (Canada).

Derby Refining Co. Accounts 65,000; cards 90,000 6 or 12 months and life. Inactive accounts 57 percent, cards 57 percent (month-to-month billing). Terms: $20–$50, 3 months; over $50, 6 months.
CHARGES: TBA, lubrication, washing, light repairs.
EXCHANGES: None.

Douglas Oil Co. of California. Accounts 90,000; cards 180,000, 6 and 24 months. Inactive accounts 50 percent, cards 50 percent (no purchase 6 months). Terms: $20 minimum, 1–3 months; up to $150, 12 months.
CHARGES: TBA, minor tune-up.
EXCHANGES: none.
UNIVERSAL CARD: Bank of America, company pays charge.

Frontier Refining Co. Accounts 37,000; cards 140,000, 3 years. Inactive accounts 8 percent, cards 40 percent (activities during prior 9 months). Terms: $15 or more, 3 to 6 months.
CHARGES: TBA, washing, lubrication.
EXCHANGES: none.

Gulf Oil Corp. Accounts 5.3 million; cards 11 million, no time limit. Inactive accounts 56 percent, cards 56 percent (no current purchases with or without a balance owing). Terms: TBA under $50 to 3 months; over $50 to 6 months; motor tune-up to 3 months $50.
CHARGES: hotel/motel, TBA, specialties, tune-ups, minor repairs, towing.
EXCHANGES: Skelly, British American Royalite.

Humble Oil & Refining Co. Inactive accounts 40 percent (do not receive a statement). Duration 2 years.
CHARGES: products supplied for resale.
EXCHANGES: Standard of Calif., Standard of Kentucky, Sohio, Sunray DX, Pure, Tidewater, Marathon, Cities Service.

Husky Oil Co. Accounts 43,000; cards 68,000, life. Inactive accounts 21 percent, cards 17.5 percent (no activity past year). Terms: $20–$50, 2 months; over $50, 6 months.
CHARGES: TBA, tire and tube repairs, wash, lubrication.

EXCHANGES: Richfield Division, Atlantic Richfield; Farmer Oil; BP Canada; Supertest, Irving; Sun (in process).

Kerr-McGee Corp. Inactive accounts. 42.6 percent (no purchase in 12 months). Duration 2 years. Terms: $20–50, 3 months; over $50, 6 months.
CHARGES: TBA service lubrication, wash, local service calls, minor repairs.
EXCHANGES: none.

Leonard Refineries Inc. Cards 30,000, 1 year. Terms: $30–$60, 3 months; $60 and over, 6 months.
CHARGES: minor repairs, TBA.
EXCHANGES: none.

Lion Oil Co. Accounts 141,000, cards 241,500, 2 years. Inactive accounts 50 percent (not used during the year). Terms: over $15, 3 months; over $50, 6 months.
CHARGES: TBA, minor repairs.
EXCHANGES: Ashland, Marathon, Pure, Signal, Tidewater, Union.
UNIVERSAL CARD: Diners Club 6 percent charge shared equally by dealer and company.

Marathon Oil Co. Accounts 502,775, cards 844,077, life. Inactive accounts 57 percent (no sales last 12 months) $15–$50, 3 months; over $50, 6 months.
CHARGES: TBA when mounted, lubrication, washing, minor repairs.
EXCHANGES: Atlantic Division, Atlantic Richfield; Humble; Lion; Supertest; Tidewater.

Mobil Oil Co. Accounts 4.5 million; cards 7.5 million, life. Inactive accounts 16 percent (no purchases last 12 months). Terms: 3, 6, 12 months.
CHARGES: TBA, minor repairs and parts, car rental, motel rooms and services.
EXCHANGES: Standard of Kentucky, Imperial, Champlin.
UNIVERSAL CARDS: American Express, Carte Blanche, Midwest Bankcharge, CAP Chargecard, Midland Charge Plan, Michigan Bankard, BankAmericard, Pittsburgh National Charge Card, Mellon Bank Card, First Wisconsin Charge Card, Connecticut Charge Card, Libertycard; company pays charges, percentage varies.

Murphy Oil Corp. Accounts 130,000, cards 260,000, 2 years. Inactive accounts 72 percent (no purchases current year). Terms: $15–$99, 6 months no charge; $100–$125, 12 months, $5 charge; $125–$150, 12 months, $6 charge.
CHARGES: TBA items.
EXCHANGES: none.
UNIVERSAL CARDS: all; company pays charge.

Oskey Brothers Petroleum Corp. Accounts 40,000, cards 55,000, life. Inactive accounts 20 percent, cards 20 percent (not used in 6 months). Terms: none.
CHARGES: miscellaneous merchandise.
EXCHANGES: none, honors all oil-company cards.

Pennzoil Co. Cards 60,000, life. Inactive cards 4 percent (not used one year). Terms: 3 months, no charge.
CHARGES: TBA, minor tune-up, small labor items, state inspections.
EXCHANGES: none.

Phillips Petroleum Co. Accounts 3.8 million, cards 6.5 million, life. Inactive accounts 60 percent, cards 60 percent (inactive at end of any month). Terms: 3–6 month, no charge.
CHARGES: TBA, repairs to $50.
EXCHANGES: Chevron, Standard of Texas, Standard of British Columbia, Signal, Imperial, Humble, Sohio, Pacific Petroleum, Tidewater, Standard of California.
UNIVERSAL CARD: Carte Blanche, Diners Club, 5 percent paid by company.

Premier Petroleum Co. Accounts 32,542; cards 65,447, 6 and 24 months. Inactive accounts 5 percent, cards 5 percent (no purchase in 6 months). Terms: up to 6 months interest free; minimum $10 monthly installments.
CHARGES: TBA mounted, minor services.
EXCHANGES: none.

Shamrock Oil & Gas Corp. Cards 575,000, life. Terms: maximum 6 months.
CHARGES: TBA, minor tune-up.
EXCHANGES: none.

Shell Oil Co. Permanent.
CHARGES: TBA, auto service and repairs, motels, insurance.
EXCHANGES: Continental, White Rose, Shell of Canada.

Signal Oil & Gas Co. Accounts 250,000; cards 450,000, 6 and 24 months. Inactive accounts 46 percent (not purchasing at all currently). Terms: 3 and 6 months.
CHARGES: TBA.
EXCHANGES: Southland Oil, Supertest, Billups Western.
UNIVERSAL CARDS: BankAmericard, 4 percent charge paid by company.

Sinclair Refining Co. Accounts over 2.5 million, cards over 6 million, 24 months. Terms: 3, 6, 9, 12 months 1.5 percent charge after 6 months.
CHARGE: TBA, minor repairs, motels, car rental, insurance, direct mail merchandise.
EXCHANGES: Atlantic Richfield, Supertest BP Canada, Irving.
UNIVERSAL CARDS: American Express, Diners, Carte Blanche; company pays charge.

Skelly Oil Co. Cards 999, 178, life.
CHARGES: TBA, food and gifts, motel.
EXCHANGES: Gulf, Tidewater, Pure, Union, Atlantic, Richfield, Sunray DX, British American, Royalite.

Standard Oil Co. of California, Western Operations Inc. Cards 4 million, 3 and 12 months. Terms: 3, 6, 9, 12 months, all with service charge.
CHARGES: TBA, normal station repairs, purchases at Ramada Inns, car rental.
EXCHANGES: Humble, Sohio, American, Sunray DX, Imperial, Irving, Chevron, Standard of Kentucky, Standard of British Columbia.

Standard Oil Co. (Kentucky). Inactive accounts 37 percent (no balance 12/31 divided by total number of customers holding cards). 3 and 12 months. Terms: 3, 6, 12 months.
CHARGES: motel and meals, Ramada Inn.
EXCHANGES: Mobil, Sohio, American Humble, Socal, Sunray DX.

Standard Oil Co. (Ohio). 2 years. Terms: 3–6 months, no charge.
CHARGES: TBA, repairs to $50.
EXCHANGES: Humble, American, Standard of California, Sunray DX, Imperial, Standard of Kentucky.

Sun Oil Co. 3 years. Terms: 3–6 months.
CHARGES: TBA, minor repairs and services.
EXCHANGES: union.
UNIVERSAL CARDS: Carte Blanche, Diners Club; company pays charges.

Sunray DX Oil Co. Accounts 834,000; cards 1.3 million, 6 months and life. Inactive accounts 66 percent, cards 54 percent (no outstanding balance, no current monthly activity).
TERMS: to 6 months, minimum $10, no charge.
CHARGES: TBA, promotional merchandise, motel.
EXCHANGES: Atlantic Richfield, Humble, Standard of Calif., Skelly, Cities Service, Sohio.

Tenneco Oil Co. Accounts 180,000; cards 350,000, life. Inactive accounts 60 percent, cards 60 percent (no purchases 6 months). Terms: $20–$50, 3 months; over $50, 3 or 6 months.
CHARGES: TBA, minor repairs, wash, lubrication.
EXCHANGES: Ashland.

Tidewater Oil Co. Accounts 225,000; 4 and 36 months. Terms: $20–$50, 3 months; 6 months and over $50.
CHARGES: TBA, minor repairs, insurance.
EXCHANGES: Pure, Pennzoil, Lion, Phillips, Irving, American Petrofina, Marathon, Home, British Petroleum, Skelly, Canadian Petrofina, Supertest.
UNIVERSAL CARDS: Carte Blanche, BankAmericard. Not honored in New York and parts of Connecticut.

Union Oil Co. of California. 4 months and life. Terms up to 15 months.
CHARGES: TBA, motels, tune-up.
EXCHANGES: Conoco, Lion, Skelly, Sun, British American, Royalite.
PURE DIVISION: Atlantic, Lion, Tidewater, Humble, Skelly, BP, Fina, Supertest.

Petroleum-Company   Appendix 5
Credit-card Tie-ins
with Motels,
Restaurants, and
Car-Rental Agencies
1967

Petroleum Company	Tie-Ins
American Oil Co.	Avis Rent a Car
	Albert Pick
	Best Eastern/Best Western
	Harvey House
	Western Motels Inc.
Atlantic Richfield Co.	Chez Bon
	Hertz Rent-A-Car
	Hyatt Hotels
	Ramada Inns
	Superior Motels
	Treadway Inn
Cities Service Oil Co.	Master Hosts
Continental Oil Co.	Master Hosts
Gulf Oil Corp.	Holiday Inns
Mobil Oil	Best Eastern/Emmons Walker
	Friendship
	Horne's
	Titan
	TraveLodge
	Treadway Inn
Phillips Petroleum Co.	Dobbs House
	Quality Courts
	Best Western
Shell Oil Co.	Sheraton Inns
Sinclair Refinery Co.	Dinkler Hotel
	Hertz Rent-A-Car
	TraveLodge
Standard Oil of California	Chez Bon
	Hertz Rent-A-Car
	Ramada Inns
Standard Oil Co. (Kentucky)	Chez Bon
	Ramada Inns
Standard Oil (Ohio)	Chez Bon
	Ramada Inns
Sun Oil Co.	Hertz Rent-A-Car

Source: "Credit-Card Tie-Ins," *1967 National Petroleum News Factbook
Issue,* mid-May 1967.

Petroleum Company	Tie-Ins
Sunray DX Oil Co.	Chez Bon Ramada Inns
Texaco Inc.	Howard Johnson Stuckey's
Union Oil Co.	American MoteLodge Master Hosts

Chapter Two

Beckhart, Benjamin Haggott. *Banking Systems*. New York: Columbia University Press, 1945.

Bolin, Sture. *State and Currency in the Roman Empire to 300* A.D. Stockholm: Almqvist and Wiksell, 1958.

"British Banks Plan Vast On-Line Networks," *Burroughs Clearing House*, May 1967.

Burns, Arthur R. *Money and Monetary Policy in Early Times*. New York: Alfred A. Knopf, 1927.

Chandler, Lester V. *The Economics of Money and Banking*. New York: Harper, 1959.

"Credit Cards — Midland's Model Army," *The Economist*, January 22, 1966.

Cumont, Franz. *The Mysteries of Mithra*. Chicago: Open Court, 1910.

Del Mar, Alexander. *A History of the Monetary Systems of France, and Other European States*. New York: Cambridge Encyclopedia, 1903.

Desmonde, William H. *Magic, Myth, and Money: The Origin of Money in Religious Ritual*. New York: Free Press of Glencoe, 1962.

Dodd, Agnes F. *History of Money in the British Empire and the United States*. London: Longmans, Green, 1911.

Ederer, Rupert J. *The Evolution of Money*. Washington, D.C.: Public Affairs Press, 1964.

Einzig, Paul. *Primitive Money*. London: Eyre-Spottiswoode, 1949.

Groseclose, Elgin. *Money and Man*. New York: Frederick Ungar, 1961.

——. *Money: The Human Conflict*. Norman: University of Oklahoma Press, 1934.

Harrison, Jane E. *Themis*. Cambridge: Cambridge at the University Press, 1927.

Hart, Albert G. "The Chicago Plan of Banking Reform," *The Review of Economic Studies*, 1935.

Hawtrey, R. G. *Currency and Credit*. London: Longmans, Green, 1919.

Kent, Raymond P. *Money and Banking*. New York: Holt, Rinehart and Winston, 1966.

Kunz, Frederick. *The Curious Lore of Precious Stones*. Philadelphia: J. B. Lippincott, 1913.

McKeon, Richard (editor). *The Basic Works of Aristotle*. New York: Random House, 1941.

Mints, Lloyd W. *A History of Banking Theory*. Chicago: University of Chicago Press, 1945.

Newlyn, W. T. *Theory of Money*. Oxford: Clarendon Press, 1962.

Nussbaum, Arthur. *A History of the Dollar*. New York: Columbia University Press, 1957.

Prather, Charles L. *Money and Banking*. 6th ed. Homewood, Ill.: Richard D. Irwin, 1957.

——. *Money and Banking*. 8th ed. Homewood: Richard D. Irwin, 1965.

Pigou, A. C. *The Veil of Money*. London: Macmillan, 1950.

Sayers, R. S. *Banking in Western Europe*. Oxford: The Clarendon Press, 1962.

Smith, Adam. *The Wealth of Nations*. New York: Modern Library Edition.

Smith, Elliot. *The Ancient Egyptians*. London: Harper, 1923.

Trescott, Paul B. *Money, Banking, and Economic Welfare*. New York: McGraw-Hill, 1965.

"This Could Mean Banking War," *The Economist*, January 15, 1966.

Thomson, F. P. *Giro Credit Transfer Systems*. Oxford: Pergamon Press, 1964.

Watson, David K. *History of American Coinage*. New York: Knickerbocker, 1899.

West, Louis C., and Allan Chester Johnson. *Currency in Roman and Byzantine Egypt*. Princeton: Princeton University Press, 1944.

Wilson, Charles Morrow. *Let's Try Barter*. New York: Devin-Adair, 1960.

Yerkes, Royden Keith. *Sacrifice in Greek and Roman Religion*. Cambridge: Cambridge at the University Press, 1908.

Chapter Three

Bagehot, Walter. *Lombard Street*. 14th ed. London: John Murray, 1915.

Board of Governors of the Federal Reserve System. *Federal Reserve Bulletin*, April 1933.

Board of Governors of the Federal Reserve System. *Federal Reserve Bulletin*, September 1935.

Board of Governors of the Federal Reserve System. *Federal Reserve Bulletin*, September 1937.

Board of Governors of the Federal Reserve System. *The Federal Reserve System Purposes and Functions*. 5th ed. Washington: Board of Governors of the Federal Reserve System, 1963.

The Constitution of the United States, Article 1, Section 8.

Dewey, D. R. *Financial History of the United States*. 10th ed. New York: Longmans, Green, 1928.

Friedman, Milton, and Anna J. Schwartz. *A Monetary History of the United States, 1867–1960*. Princeton: Princeton University Press for the National Bureau of Economic Research, 1963.

Hepburn, Barton. *History of Coinage in the United States.* New York: Macmillan, 1930.

Lerner, E. M. "Inflation in the Confederacy, 1861–1865," in Milton Friedman (ed.), *Studies in the Quantity Theory of Money,* Chicago: University of Chicago Press, 1956.

Murphy, H. C. *The National Debt in War and Transition.* New York: McGraw-Hill, 1950.

Nussbaum, Arthur. *A History of the Dollar.* New York: Columbia University Press, 1957.

O'Connor, J. F. T. *The Banking Crisis and Recovery under the Roosevelt Administration.* Chicago: Callaghan, 1938.

Prather, Charles L. *Money and Banking.* 8th ed. Homewood, Ill.: Richard D. Irwin, 1965.

The Story of Checks. 2nd ed. New York: The Federal Reserve Bank of New York, 1962.

Chapter Four

Anderson, Allan H., and others. *An Electronic Cash and Credit System.* New York: American Management Association, 1966.

Board of Governors of the Federal Reserve System. *Federal Reserve Bulletin,* January 1968.

"Federal Reserve to Install Computerized Wire Links," *The Wall Street Journal,* February 28, 1968.

Hawtrey, R. G. *Currency and Credit.* London: Longmans, Green, 1919.

Ludtke, James B. *The American Financial System.* 2nd ed. Boston: Allyn and Bacon, 1961.

Sitomer, Daniel. "The Check — Its Role in the Checkless Society," in *Proceedings National Automation Conference,* New York: The American Bankers Association, 1967.

The Story of Checks. 2nd ed. New York: The Federal Reserve Bank of New York, 1962.

Systems, Standards and Information Processing Group. *The Check in Perspective.* New York: The Chase Manhattan Bank, N. A., 1967.

Chapter Five

"Boosting Credit Card Sales," *National Petroleum News,* March, 1957.

"Breakdown of Oil-Company Credit-Card Accounts," *1967 National Petroleum News Factbook Issue,* mid-May 1967.

Correspondence with Mr. Sam Flanel, Vice President, National Retail Merchants Association, February 29, 1968.

"Credit-Card Bonanza — and the Cost of Exploiting It," *National Petroleum News,* October 1964.

"Credit Card Companies Come into the Chips," *Business Week,* September 4, 1965.

"Credit Card Firm Seeks New Life," *National Petroleum News,* March 31, 1954.

"Credit Card Kaleidoscope," *Financial World,* December 15, 1965.

"Credit-Card Merchandising: Can It Stop the Cost Spiral?" *National Petroleum News,* October 1964.

"Credit Cards Are Here to Stay," *Financial World,* March 27, 1963.

"Credit Card Shakeout," *Financial World,* January 13, 1965.

"Credit-Card Tie-Ins," *1967 National Petroleum News Factbook Issue,* mid-May 1967.

"Credit Costs — and Costs More for Smaller Stores," *Stores,* March 1965.

"Credit-Swapping at Car Washes Bothers Majors in Los Angeles," *National Petroleum News,* July 1966.

Due, Jean M. "Consumer Knowledge of Installment Credit Charges," *Journal of Marketing,* October 1955.

"Expanded Use of Oil Credit Cards," *National Petroleum News,* December 1964.

"How a Private-Brand Jobber Controls Credit-Card Costs," *National Petroleum News,* April 1964.

"Is That Credit Card Any Good?" *National Petroleum News,* November 1965.

Juster, F. Thomas, "Consumer Sensitivity to the Price of Credit," *The Journal of Finance,* May 1964.

"Lagging Leader," *Forbes,* October 15, 1965.

"Machines Move Mountains for Paper-Ridden Marathon," *National Petroleum News,* September 1966.

"New Ideas Are Coming Fast," *National Petroleum News,* December 1957.

"New Revolution in Credit-Card Processing," *National Petroleum News,* November 1965.

"New Shuffle in Credit Cards," *Business Week,* November 3, 1962.

"Oils Credity Puzzle: How to Get Million to Use Their Cards," *National Petroleum News,* June 1967.

Richardson, D. W. "Technological Innovation in the Future of Commercial Banking," *Business Studies,* North Texas State University, Fall 1967.

"Tougher Going for Credit Cards," *Business Week,* September 4, 1965.

"Universal Card Ready," *The Oil and Gas Journal,* June 20, 1960.

"Universal Credit Card," *National Petroleum News,* November 19, 1952.

"What Scanners Are Doing for Humble," *National Petroleum News,* November 1965.

"What 10 Companies Are Doing, What They Sell, How, To Whom," *National Petroleum News,* October 1964.

"Where Credit-Card Buying Is Headed," *The Oil and Gas Journal,* September 9, 1959.

Chapter Six

"Bank of America Says Use of Its Credit Card Rose in '67," *The Wall Street Journal,* January 10, 1968.

Banks, Richard V., Vice-President, First National City Bank, New York, New York. Presentation before the American Bankers Association's Preauthorized Payments Workshop, New Orleans, Louisiana, January 25–26, 1968.

Cantor, Carl W., Vice-President, First National Bank of Canton, Canton, Ohio. Presentation before the American Bankers Association's Preauthorized Payments Workshop, New Orleans, Louisiana, January 25–26, 1968.

"Careless Issuance of Credit Cards by Banks Stirs Federal Reserve Worry over Risks," *The Wall Street Journal*, August 21, 1967.

Carter, Duncan G. "Today's Decisions for Progress and Profit in Credit Card Banking," Address before the Annual Bank Operations — NABAC Conference, April 5, 1967.

"Charge Accounts at the Chase," *Business Week*, October 25, 1958.

"The Charge-It Plan That Really Took Off," *Business Week*, February 2, 1965.

Correspondence with Mr. Charles A. Brackenbury, Coordinator of Sales and Services, BankAmericard Center, Pasadena, California, July 17, 1967.

Correspondence with Mr. Duncan G. Carter, Assistant Vice-President and Manager Charge Account Service, First National Bank and Trust Company of Kalamazoo, Michigan, July 20, 1967.

Correspondence with Mr. Steven A. Vanden Bergh, Vice-President, Franklin National Bank, New York, July 31, 1967.

"Credit," *Time*, April 21, 1967.

"Credit Card Kaleidoscope," *Financial World*, December 15, 1965.

"Electronic Money," *Forbes*, April 1, 1967.

Federal Reserve Bank of Boston, *Functional Cost Analysis*, 1961 and 1962.

Lowther, George E., Assistant Vice-President, Wells Fargo Bank, San Francisco, California. Presentation before the American Bankers Association's Preauthorized Payments Workshop, New Orleans, Louisiana, January 25–26, 1968.

Rabn, Gary B., Vice-President, First Wisconsin National Bank of Milwaukee. Presentation before the American Bankers Association's Preauthorized Payments Workshop, New Orleans, Louisiana, January 25–26, 1968.

A Summary of the Feasibility Determination and Implementation Plan Report for a Common Bank Credit Card Plan (Prepared for Bank of California, N.A., Croker Citizens National Bank, United California Bank, and Wells Fargo Bank by Information Sciences Associates, Cherry Hill, New Jersey), September 19, 1966.

"Throwing in the Sponge," *Forbes*, February 1, 1962.

Towey, Richard E. "An Evaluation of the Payments Mechanism in California, 1946–1975," in Hyman P. Minsky, *California Banking in a Growing Economy: 1946–1975*, Berkeley: Institute of Business and Economic Research, University of California, 1965.

"US 'Instant Money Game' Increasingly 'Played' Today," (UPI), *Austin American Statesman*, November 5, 1967.

Chapter Seven

Hawtrey, R. G. *Currency and Credit*. London: Longmans Green, 1919, Chapter 1.

Chapter Eight

Anderson, Allan H., and others. *An Electronic Cash and Credit System*. New York: American Management Association, 1966. Chapter 4.

Axelson, Kenneth S., Vice-President/Director of Finance and Administration, J. C. Penney Company, Inc., New York. Presentation before the National Credit-Card Conference of the American Bankers Association, Chicago, Illinois, November 9, 1967.

Cary, A. K. "Our Moneyless Society," *Burroughs Clearing House*, March 1960.

"Electronic Money," *Forbes*, April 1, 1967.

"Hard Figures and Considered Judgments on Progress Towards Checkless Society," *American Banker*, February 17, 1967.

Mathews, Richard S. "The Role of Other Industries in a Checkless Society" (unpublished manuscript).

Mitchell, George W. "Effects of Automation on the Structure and Functioning of Banking," *The American Economic Review*, May 1966.

Phelps, Clyde W. *Accounts Receivable Financing As a Method of Business Finance*, Studies in Commercial Financing, No. 2, Commercial Credit Company (1957).

——. *The Role of Factoring in Modern Business Finance*, Studies in Commercial Finance No. 1, Commercial Credit Company, 1956.

Reistad, Dale L. "The Coming Cashless Society," *Business Horizons*, Fall 1967.

Richardson, D. W. *Payment Media Systems Innovation: The Prospects for the Banking Industry*. Austin: The College of Business Administration, The University of Texas at Austin, July, 1967, Research Paper 67–16.

Roth, Arthur T., Chairman and Chief Executive, Franklin National Bank of New York. Presentation before the National Credit-Card Conference of the American Bankers Association, Chicago, Illinois, November 9, 1967.

Smith, William D. "The Checkless Society: Human Beings Causing the Chief Delays," *The New York Times*, May 21, 1967, Section 3.

"Stepping Stones to the Checkless Society," *Burroughs Clearing House*, June 1967.

Westrup, William H. "Needed: A Central Source for Consumer Credit Data," *Burrough Clearing House*, December 1966.

Woodley, Annette Pike, and H. Ellsworth Steele. "Charge Account Banking in the Sixth Federal Reserve District," *Atlanta Economic Review*, November 1966.

Chapter Nine

Baumol, William J. "The Transactions Demand for Cash; An Inventory Theoretic Approach," *The Quarterly Journal of Economics*, 1952.

Birnbaum, Eugene A. "The Growth of Financial Intermediaries as a

Factor in the Effectiveness of Monetary Policy," *Staff Papers,* International Monetary Fund, VI, November 1958.

Friedman, Milton. *A Program for Monetary Stability.* New York: Fordham University Press, 1960.

Gurley, John G., and Edward S. Shaw. *Money in a Theory of Finance.* Washington, D.C.: The Brookings Institution, 1960.

Hastings, Delbert C., and Ross M. Robertson. "The Mysterious World of the Fed," *Business Horizons,* Spring 1962.

Kareken, John, and Robert M. Solow. "Lags in Monetary Policy: A Summary," in *Stabilization Policies.* Commission on Money and Credit. Englewood Cliffs, Prentice-Hall, 1963.

Keynes, John Maynard. *General Theory of Employment, Interest and Money.* London: St. Martins, 1936.

Meltzer, Allan H. "Monetary Policy and the Trade Credit Practices of Business Firms," in *Stabilization Policies,* Commission on Money and Credit. Englewood Cliffs, N.J.: Prentice-Hall, 1963.

Money and Credit: Their Influence on Jobs, Prices, and Growth, The Report of the Commission on Money and Credit. Englewood Cliffs, N.J.: Prentice-Hall, 1961.

Richardson, D. W. "The Potential Impact of Technical Innovations in Commercial Banking on the Transactions Demand for Money Balances," *Marquette Business Review,* Winter 1967.

Schlesinger, James R. "Monetary Policy and Its Critics," *Journal of Political Economy,* December 1960.

Shapiro, Robert. "Financial Intermediaries, Credit Availability, and Aggregate Demand," *Journal of Finance,* September 1966.

Shelby, Donald. "Some Implications of the Growth of Financial Intermediaries," *Journal of Finance,* December, 1958.

Thorn, Richard S. "Nonbank Financial Intermediaries, Credit Expansion, and Monetary Policy," *Staff Papers,* International Monetary Fund, VI, November 1958.

Tobin, James. "The Interest-Elasticity of Transactions Demand for Cash," *The Review of Economics and Statistics,* August 1956.

United States Joint Economic Committee. *Employment, Growth, and Price Levels, Hearings.* Part 6C, 86th Congress, 1st Session. Washington, D.C.: Government Printing Office, 1959.

Miscellaneous

Bright, James R. *Research, Development, and Technological Innovation.* Homewood, Richard D. Irwin, 1964.

Bronfenbrenner, Martin, and Thomas Mayer. "Liquidity Functions in the American Economy," *Ecometrica,* October 1960.

Brunner, Karl, and Allan H. Meltzer. "Predicting Velocity: Implications for Theory and Policy," *The Journal of Finance,* May 1963.

Credit Card and Revolving Credit Survey. New York: Installment Credit Committee, The American Bankers Association, 1967.

Eisner, Robert. "Another Look at Liquidity Preference," *Econometrica,* July 1963.

Friedman, Milton. *The Demand for Money: Some Theoretical and Em-*

pirical Results. New York: National Bureau of Economic Research, 1959.

Hansen, Alvin H. *Monetary Theory and Fiscal Policy.* New York: McGraw-Hill, 1949.

Haywood, Charles F. "Hoarding, Velocity, and Financial Intermediaries," *The Southern Economic Journal,* May 1966.

Isenson, Raymond S. "Technological Forecasting a Management Tool," *Business Horizons,* Summer 1967.

Johnson, Herbert E., Vice-President and Economist, Continental Illinois National Bank and Trust Company of Chicago. "Banking and Automation — Implications for Bank Management," Conference on Banking in the Next Decade, Princeton University, Princeton, New Jersey, December 7, 1967.

Kramer, Robert L., and W. Putnam Livingston. "Cashing In on the Checkless Society," *Harvard Business Review,* September–October 1967.

Lee, Tong Hun. "Substitutability of Non-Bank Intermediary Liabilities for Money: The Empirical Evidence," *The Journal of Finance,* No. 3, September 1966.

Meltzer, Allan H. "The Demand for Money: A Cross-Section Study of Business Firms," *The Quarterly Journal of Economics,* August 1963.

——. "The Demand for Money: The Evidence from the Time Series," *Journal of Political Economy,* June 1963.

Mitchell, George W. "Governor Mitchell Considers Tomorrow's Banking," *Banking,* December 1966.

Morrison, George R. "Deposit Structure, the Price Level, and Bank Earnings," *The National Banking Review,* December 1964.

Morton, Jack A. "A Systems Approach to the Innovation Process," *Business Horizons,* Summer 1967.

O'Connor, J. F. T. *Banks under Roosevelt.* Chicago: Callaghan, 1938.

Patinkin, Don. *Money, Interest, and Prices.* New York: Harper and Row, 1965.

Shapiro, Robert. "Financial Intermediaries, Credit Availability, and Aggregate Demand," *The Journal of Finance,* September 1966.

Shatto, Gloria. "Money Substitutes for the Corporate Business Sector," *The Journal of Finance,* March 1967.

Silverberg, Stanley. "Profitability of Commercial Bank Time Deposits," *The National Banking Review,* December 1963.

"Soon You'll Never See Money at All," *Changing Times,* October 1967.

Sprenkle, Case M. "Is the Precautionary Demand for Money Negative?" *The Journal of Finance,* March 1967.

——. "Large Economic Units, Banks, and the Transactions Demand for Money," *The Quarterly Journal of Economics,* August 1966.

A Techno-Economic Study of Methods of Improving the Payments Mechanism. Stanford Research Institute, December 1966.

Teigen, Ronald L. "Demand and Supply Functions for Money in the United States: Some Structural Estimates," *Econometrica,* October 1964.

Whalen, Edward L. "A Rationalization of the Precautionary Demand for Cash," *The Quarterly Journal of Economics,* May 1966.

Name Index